To Jay —
One of my
greatest
fans,
with love
John Palmer

World-wide Praise for the Erotica of John Patrick!

"This writing is what being brave is all about. It brings up the kinds of things that are usually kept so private that you think you're the only one who experiences them."

"Tantalizing tales of porn stars, hustlers, and other lost boys...John Patrick set the pace with 'Angel!'"
- Jesse Monteagudo, The Weekly News, Miami

"...Some readers may find some of the scenes too explicit; others will enjoy the sudden, graphic sensations each page brings. Each of these romans á clef is written with sustained intensity. 'Angel' offers a strange, often poetic vision of sexual obsession. I recommend it to you."
- Noveau Midwest

"Self-absorbed, sexually-addicted bombshell Stacy flounced onto the scene in 'Angel' and here he is again, engaged in further, distinctly 'non-literary' adventures ...lots of action!"
- Prinz Eisenherz Book Review, Germany

"...'Billy & David' is frank, intelligent, sometimes disarming. Few books approach the government's failure to respond to crisis in such a realistic, powerful manner."
- RG Magazine, Montreal, Canada

Book of the Month Selections in Europe and the U.K. Featured Selections at A Different Light, Lambda Rising and GR, Australia

The KiD

The Confessions of a Rock Star's Secret Young Lover

A Shocking Love Story by
JOHN PATRICK

With Joe Leslie

STARbooks Press
Sarasota, FL

Books by John Patrick
Non-Fiction
The Best of the Superstars 1990
A Charmed Life: Vince Cobretti
Lowe Down: Tim Lowe
The Best of the Superstars 1991
Legends: The World's Sexiest Men, Vol. 1
The Best of the Superstars 1992
What Went Wrong? When Boys Are Bad & Sex Goes Wrong

Fiction
Billy & David: A Deadly Minuet
The Bigger They Are...
The Younger They Are...
The Harder They Are...
Angel: The Complete Trilogy
Angel II: Stacy's Story
Angel: The Complete Quintet
A Natural Beauty (Ed.)
The Kid (with Joe Leslie)
STRIP: He Danced Alone
Huge (Ed.)

Library of Congress Card Catalogue No. 91-067530
ISBN No. 1 877978-27-2

I Knew This Kid

I knew this skinny little kid
  Who never wanted to play tackle football at all
But thought he'd better if he wanted
  His daddy to love him and to prove his courage
And things like that.
  I remember him holding his breath
And closing his eyes
  And throwing a block into a guy twice his size
Proving he was brave enough to be loved, and crying softly
  Because his tailbone hurt
And his shoes were so big they made him stumble.

I knew this skinny little kid
  With sky-blue eyes and soft brown hair
Who liked cattails and pussy willows,
  Sumac huts and sassafras.
Who liked chestnuts and pine cones and oily walnuts,
  Lurking foxes and rabbits munching lilies,
Secret caves and moss around the roots of oaks,
  Beavers and muskrats and gawking herons.
And I wonder what he would have been
  If someone had loved him for
Just following the fawns and building waterfalls
  And watching the white rats have babies.
I wonder what he would have been
  If he hadn't played tackle football at all.

- James Kavanaugh
"Will You Be My Friend?"
Published by
Steven J. Nash

"I love comebacks. Of course, the best way to make a comeback is not leave in the first place."

- Joe Skinner

Prologue

"I'll show ya how, kid," Kenny said.

And, as simple as that, a new way of life started for me. "Most of the older dudes wanta blow ya or want your prick up their ass. They like to get fucked by a young, good lookin' stud. Some of 'em'll wanta screw ya, too, and if they do, charge 'em more. Lots more." I nodded. That'll be the day, I thought, when I let anybody stick anything up my ass.

When we arrived at his little furnished room up three flights of stairs, I told him I felt like I needed a shower and he said he wanted to bathe me. Well, okay, I thought, I can act like a baby if that's what turns him on. He soaped me all over very carefully in a kind of neutral way, not lingering anywhere except maybe to massage my nipples and then he dried me with a big towel as if he were my mother. After he had rubbed me dry, he found some oil and had me lie on my stomach on the bed and he went over me very slowly, deliberately, starting at my shoulders and then moving on, down my spine, over my hips and ass, then sliding his hand in, down between my legs until I squirmed. I couldn't believe it but I had an erection. As he was massaging the soles of my feet, I was ready to come.

I reached down and stroked my cock. "Hey, wait," he said. "Wait for me."

He rolled me over and climbed onto the bed, his knees between my legs, pushing them apart to make a V. Then he put his hand down, rubbing my prick and balls. "Yeah, ya got a helluva nice big one. Make it work for ya, never settle for less'n twenty."

His lips rested gently on mine. It wasn't really a kiss, just lips touching lips. Then his tongue moved to the right side of my chest, then the left, then down, finally coming to rest on the head of my cock. I ran my fingers through his hair. He flicked his tongue around the head of my cock and then swallowed the whole thing, down to the pubic hairs. "Oh, shit," I cried, moving my hips upward.

He slid his hands under my raised ass and a finger began to probe my asshole. He kept sucking, expertly, until I was ready again; then he pulled away. "Never rush the guy. Ya never know who might become your sugar daddy." He climbed off the bed and started to undress.

I watched intently as his shorts dropped to the floor. I sighed when I saw his cock. It was smaller than mine but it seemed much more elegant, perfectly shaped, standing out like a rose in full bloom. I'd never seen a prettier one.

"Now, you try it," he said, stroking it.

Seconds before, I was hornier than I'd ever been in my life, but my cock went soft. I shook.

"Just lick it," he instructed. I tried it. It tasted good. I made out like I wasn't in any hurry but I was. He groaned a little. It was not so much from pleasure as impatience. He nudged me and I began to suck him the way he had sucked me. The more of it I took in, the more I wanted. But I let it slide from my mouth so I could lick the wiry hair on his balls and feel the weight of them as they lolled against my tongue. Then I moved up to the crease between his balls and thigh to the very root of his sweet dick. I toyed with the hair at the base of his cock, then moved a few inches where his belly began, soft, hairy. I found his navel and nuzzled my nose in it. He groaned again. I could feel him tense with excitement as I lowered my head and took the shaft between my lips.

He began thrusting it into me and I held on. "Oh, yeah. But hold it. Take it easy. We ain't even halfway through the lesson."

And he pulled away again and lit a cigarette. I lay there, silent, stroking myself, watching him pushing smoke rings to the ceiling. "Yeah, you're a pretty one all right. You'll do good. Nice cock, decent bod. Yeah, you'll make it."

When he finished his cigarette, he took some lube from the drawer and applied it on my cock. "Shit, man, guys are really gonna love this - " It crossed my mind maybe he was speaking for himself more than anyone else, so anxious was he to lower himself over it, have it in him. He tilted his head back and closed his eyes. I just lay there, letting him guide it in. As he bounced up and down on it for a while, I enjoyed the sensations of the energy that hovered over me, taking me in, then out. "Oh, yeah!" he cried.

Soon he was lifting himself off, away from me and lying back down on the bed. He spread his legs wide and I got between them.

He took my slick cock in his hand and guided it in again. When it was all the way in, he grabbed my ass and held me tightly.

I began. It seemed like every part of my body was singing. I could see my prick, then I couldn't. His hard stomach muscles rippled as he worked his ass in a fury beneath me. The hair of his legs, now resting on my shoulders, caressed each side of my face.

The way I look at it, when your meat's up and pressing, straining, does it matter where it goes? I'd fucked a couple of cunts back in Ohio but this, this was different. He knew how to touch, how to stroke, to get a guy so horny there'd be a real show. After all, he said, it was his business. He saw me getting off the bus and offered to carry my suitcase. It was as if he was expecting me. In a way, he was. "I like to get 'em when they're fresh," he told me after buying me dinner. "I was fresh once myself."

The sensations I was feeling were so new, so foreign. The tightness sort of hurt at first, then, as the whole length of my cock settled into him, it was warm, moist, and it seemed it was inviting me to linger there. But I didn't. I withdrew, but quickly plunged back in. Dazed, I just kept on, calmly, almost mechanically. When I opened my eyes, I saw him smiling, watching me as I worked over him. Gently he moved his hands up and down my arms, then massaged my neck and left his hands there, still watching, enjoying the view, moaning low. I took his cock in my hand and stroked it. It wasn't long before he was coming and I realized I was coming, too. But even after I shot my load, I was still hard and not ready to stop. He just groaned, closed his eyes and held me as I kept on.

It was a long night, perhaps the longest of my young life.

From the LP "I Remember You"/Sung by Joe Skinner/Side 1, Cut 1, "I Remember You:" "...You're the one who made my dreams come true / A few kisses ago / I remember you / You're the one who said / I love you, too / I do, didn't you know? / Oh, I remember, too / A distant bell / And stars that fell / Like rain / Out of the blue / When my life is through / And the angels ask me to recall / That thrill of them all / Then I shall tell them / I remember you."

"Ya gotta advertise, man. Kid like you could get killed on the street." That was Kenny's advice. So he helped me run an ad. And got me a beeper. I was in business.

"Photo. Ya gotta run a fuckin' photo," Kenny told me later when I bitched because we got only two calls. "Kid like you, shit, it's all in the photo. Let 'em see some of what they're gonna get."

I didn't have a fucking photo; nothing but a couple of Polaroids a guy took of me once. But a guy who picked me up on the street one time told me if I ever needed some photos, he'd even pay me to pose. I searched for the business card for three days and finally found it. "John D. Strange, Master Photographer." That's all it said, with the phone number in tiny type. I called.

Strange said he didn't remember me but if he'd given me his card, I had to be a hot number so he agreed to see me. I took a cab to the address on Sunset, way out, almost to the ocean.

"...Oh, yes, how could I forget?" he laughed when he saw me, then he groped me.

"I just need a shot to put with my ad," I said, pulling away. If he wanted it, he was going to have to pay.

"A whole layout or nothing."

"I dunno." I started to get the hell outta there.

"I'll tell you what," he said, moving close again, touching my shoulder. "I'm a fair man. I don't take advantage of boys. I'll be able to get several hundred dollars for a layout on you. 'In Touch,' 'Advocate Men,' one of 'em'll eat it up. So, you spend the night and I'll give you the photo you need, with a negative, and I'll throw in a hundred-dollar tip. How's that sound?"

I took his hand and placed it on my groin. "Like fuckin' music to my ears."

And fucking, not music, was certainly what he had in mind. "That blow job I gave you in my car, parked on that side street, that was just for starters," he said, finally remembering.

He took me to his house, a comfortable little place in Malibu. He decided I would look best in a bed and he had the perfect one for it, a round one with pink silk sheets and funny pillows with lace on them. He said he wanted to soften my "stud" look and I said, "Sure." I was used to being whatever the john wanted. Kenny had taught me that. He had me playing every role, even dressing in drag. He got off eating my asshole out when I had black lace nylons on and a nightie. It blew my mind.

Strange wanted me to be a sissy, too, I knew that right off. It began with the make-up. There had to be make-up. He said, "No imperfections in my pictures."

It took him an hour to get it all right. The lip gloss was the crowning touch.

But it was more than just for the pictures. He wanted to have a real sissy fuck him. I couldn't figure it. Pose, pose, then jab, jab. It got to be boring as hell but I played along.

We stopped for dinner. He wanted to take me out. "I want to show you off to my friends," he said.

When we were seated at a cozy table at the Sandbar, he ordered drinks and then toasted me. "To my next star."

"Me, a star? You gotta be crazy!"

"Oh, it won't be the first time a photo layout of mine has led to a kid becoming a movie star."

"Yeah, who?"

"Jeff Bailey, for one."

"Never heard of 'im."

"How many gay videos do you watch in a week? In a month?"

"None."

"Well, see. How would you know him? But he's big, I'll tell you that. He posed for me two years ago and now he's made ten videos. When we get back to the house I'll show you one."

Looking at Jeff Bailey I couldn't believe anybody would want to fuck him much less take a picture of him or put him in a video. Strange went on and on about him, though, and I just couldn't figure it. Maybe he gave great head but you couldn't tell it by the video. Then Strange told me what must have been Bailey's secret. "He can get it up just like that," he said, snapping his fingers. "Never fails. They call him 'ever ready.'"

I can do that, I thought. Kenny taught me. When I'm with a trick I don't like, all I have to do is close my eyes and think of Kenny and I get hard. Just the thought of fucking him and bang! It's unreal but it works every time. But then, after a while, I have to open my eyes and reality kicks in and it's a struggle, especially when they get greedy, even after you've come and they've come, they want more. Always more. More and more these days, I have to think of Kenny. And not just fucking Kenny, either. Sometimes, suckin' him. That cock that could only be described as elegant. They go on and on about my cock, but Kenny's cock, that's the prize.

Strange had some silk panties that matched the sheets and he had me slip them on. He liked sucking me through the fabric until I was hard, then bent over at the waist. He watched in the mirror as I slid my cock and balls across his ass. He moaned, loving the feel of the silk against his skin, "Oh, honey. Honey, honey, honey."

I slipped the silk down and shoved my cock between his cheeks. As I entered him, he cried, "Oh, baby. God, it's so big - I can't take it. I can't! I...Oh, it feels so good."

Jacking off as I slammed into him, he screamed, "You're such a little queen, but you have such a big dick! Oh, fuck me, fuck me raw, baby, I love it."

When he came, he said, "Oh, you little fairies know how to fuck." I couldn't fuckin' figure it but I wasn't being paid to figure it.

After dinner, we started the whole routine over again, only with lighting, lighting all over the place. I'd pose, then he'd suck me and get it up, then shoot some more, then bend over. I'd do it for awhile, then it was back to shooting again until he decided he'd had plenty of poses.

I'd agreed to stay the night but I was so anxious to see the photos that I begged him to take the film to the studio and develop them. He had shot a roll of black and white just for me so that was what he processed, first as a proof sheet. There were 36 pictures, each one better than the other. He really was good, I had to admit it. I didn't know which one to pick so he suggested three. He said the magazine wouldn't run a full nude anyway so he decided to make a print just for them. Trimming me right below my belly button, he laughed, "I'm cropping out your best feature but that's the way it is. They'll have to pay to see it."

*

And pay they did. I had ten calls the first day and it kept getting busier. It was so busy, I was glad that just after I had gotten here I'd done all the stuff I'd always wanted to do if I ever visited L.A., like go to the Walk of Fame and the Chinese Theater and see some TV shows being filmed. I even went downtown on the bus to see them film a scene for a movie at the Park Plaza hotel. But the reality of it didn't impress me. Somebody working the lights told me that they were spending an entire day on a scene that would take less than two minutes in the actual movie, just Dudley Moore running into the hotel and into an elevator. I figured I had better things to do, like watch the movies on my TV.

Then I got a call from a guy who said his name was Van and he said he ran "the best damn escort service in the country, the Beverly Hills All-Stars." He said Kenny had told him all about me and he knew I was one of "his kind" of boys. I made an appointment for the next day.

From the LP "I Remember You" /Sung by Joe Skinner/Side One, Cut Two, "I Won't Send Roses:" "*My heart is too much in control | The lack of romance in my soul | Will turn you gray, kid | So stay away, kid | Forget my shoulder | When you're in need | Forgetting birthdays is guaranteed | And should I love you | You would be the last to know | I won't send roses | And roses suit you so.*"

"Gorgeous ass," Van said as I turned around, displaying myself for him. "My clients'll love plugging that."

"I don't get fucked."

"Everybody says that at first."

"No. I just don't. Never will."

"Well, it's a pity. Ass like that could go for two hundred easy. Maybe more."

"Gettin' fucked is for queers."

He brought his pudgy fingers to his lips. "I'm sure you've heard the expression, 'Yesterday's trade—'"

"Yeah, but I ain't trade. I know trade. It's just that, well, the idea of gettin' fucked is such a turn-off for me. I've had guys try it and I just couldn't handle it."

"I would have loved to have been there," he murmured.

"Yeah, I guess you would've had to have been there all right."

"I meant, I've been around a long time. Seen everything." He ran his hand across his bald head. "You were just scared. Maybe I could have helped the situation."

"Nobody could've helped that situation, believe me."

"Well, in today's world, you can get by very easily never even pulling your pants down. It's a whole different scene than it was when I started in this business back in the '70s."

He went on and on and I tuned out, looking about the room, a shabby place with funny little cats running all around. Beverly Hills my ass.

"Yeah, well," I said, finally, remembering an old movie I saw once, "Hell's Angels," "my philosophy is like Jean Harlow's."

"Oh?"

"Yeah, she said, 'Life's short and I want to live while I'm alive.'"

"I hope you do. The more living you do, the more money I'll make."

He'd hold one cat, pet it for awhile, then it'd leave and another one would jump on his lap. I knew I would be calling him Catman before long. "Van the Catman," I giggled.

"What?"

"Oh, nothin'. You sure love your cats."

"Only kind of lovin' I can get any more. Sad, isn't it?"

I understood him completely. On the farm, the animals were my lovers. I had a cat once, too, before the girl down the road dropped it over the back staircase so that his skull cracked. And we'd been told cats always landed on their feet.

"Shit, what you talkin' about? I mean, you got all these boys."

"Oh, my no! After the first interview, I never see my boys again. They pick up their money from the box downstairs. They hardly ever make it back up here. You, on the other hand, you could come up any time."

"How do you know? You ain't even seen the best part of me."

"Kenny told me but, okay, if you're so proud of it, show me. But slowly, so I can enjoy it. I won't touch. I don't touch any more. Sad, isn't it?"

I didn't answer. By my silence I was agreeing with him about how sad everything was for him and that's why I wanted to give him some pleasure right at this moment, so I loosened the zipper and lowered it slowly, like he told me to, moving closer to where he was sitting on the couch. As I pushed the jeans down my hips my cock slipped out, then my balls. I stood there, not moving.

"Oh, god, it is pretty. How big does it get?"

I closed my eyes and thought about Kenny. My cock sprang to full attention.

"Wow!" He swallowed hard. "Step just a bit closer."

His hand left the cat's spine and stroked my cock, as if he was petting it, too.

"My oh my, what I would have done with that in the old days. Hmmm." He gently squeezed my balls. "Such a stud. Such a stud." His hand returned to his cat, who was purring loudly. "Oh, I've heard about you, you know. I was curious how long it would take Kenny to start advertising you. Well, you can forget Kenny, forget all of that now. You're working exclusively for me. You go where

I say and do as I say and we'll be fine. There's not many that can get it up no matter what."

"Yeah, no matter what."

"Okay, you can put it away."

I was suddenly glad he didn't want me to perform for him. I'd had fatter, uglier johns before, but there was something about him that was beginning to turn my stomach, even if he did like animals.

"For a kid like you, there's films, too, you know. There's one shooting right now just down the street. All you'd have to do is go onto the set, pull it out and let three guys give you head. Want me to book you?"

"How much?" I asked, stuffing myself back into my jeans.

"Two fifty. But only if you come for the camera."

I didn't hesitate a second. "I'll take it."

From the LP "I Remember You" / Sung by Joe Skinner / Side 1, Cut 3, "Easy to Love:" "...You'd be so easy to love / So easy to idolize all others above... We'd be so grand at the game / So carefree together / That it does seem a shame / That you can't see your future with me / Because you'd be, oh, so easy to love."

The Catman was right. It was the easiest thing I'd ever done. I just walked onto what they called a set, something out of one of those movies that they're always saying are the worst ones ever made, like "Plan Nine from Outer Space." I walked right up to the man with the camera, an ugly man in his mid 30's with fuzzy hair. "I've been a movie fan all my life," I told him, and he just stared at me as if I wasn't there.

"Just take your clothes off, kid and put this on," the director yelled at me.

"And be quick about it, we ain't got all day, you know."

So much for learning about movie-making, if you could call that movie-making.

He handed me a little silver bikini and after I was ready, I was told to walk through this dry ice as if I was from outer space, visiting these three guys on a spaceship. There were no preliminaries. They were all over me, yanking my bikini off and sliding down on their knees around me and going at it. I was more interested in what was happening alongside us, the taping of it, than I was the action.

It took less than an hour for them to shoot me having my cock blown. The fuzzy haired man must have taken it from every angle six times. When I came, they went nuts. The guys kept kissing me all over while they jacked off. When everybody had come, the director talked about another movie the following week. "You're good, kid," he said.

I signed a release and got my fee in cash. "Hey," the assistant, a skinny guy named Jerry, yelled as I was leaving, "what name do you wanta go by?"

I was startled. I didn't think I'd have my name in the credits or anything.

He laughed, "Not that it makes any fuckin' difference because they'll probably change it anyway, but we always ask."

"My name's William, William Kidd. But they've always just called me 'kid.' Like in, 'Hey, you kid' or Billy the Kid. Yeah, that's it, just call me 'The Kid.'"

*

Three days later, the Catman got me another job. He asked me if I could fuck a woman as well as I fucked a man. "Sure," I said.

...Brandy came to the set in a little black tube of a skirt and high black boots and a tank top held to the skirt by teeny suspenders, creating the impression that her whole body was in a garter belt. It was an outfit that backhome would have the local boys hanging out of their car windows and howling at her. The director got her topless right off.

The first scene had me on my back and her doing what they called a backwards cowgirl. Brandy didn't want to do it. "Yuck! It's so unnatural. His dick goes one way, my body goes the other. And with a cock that big, it'll hurt." But the director said that's what they wanted and she had to do it. "Great view of the action," he said as he prepared to film it. She blew me a while and then did her thing. They said I didn't have to come until the next scene but she went through all sorts of gyrations making believe she had six or seven orgasms.

"...This ain't the job I dreamed about in college," she told me matter-of-factly while we are waiting for the other guy to arrive to film the next scene. "Can you imagine what it's like to tell people you just made a movie called 'The Slut?'"

"No, I can't imagine." I wanted to tell her about the movie I made last week but I didn't. I didn't want her to think I was carrying some kind of virus.

"...I told my daddy; I says, look, Pa, nobody pays me to sit at home. First I was in a John Robert Powers Modelling School but there was this ugly bitch with five facelifts tellin' ya how to walk with an umbrella and how to get in and outta a car. I mean, let's get real."

"Not what you planned, eh?"

"Honey, I never make a plan, " she winked. "I kinda think whatever happens, happens; you know what I mean?"

"Yeah, I sure do."

She went on talking. She said she loved to shop in thrift stores. I told her that's the only place I ever shopped and we sort of hit it off right then. And she was crushed that the pair of huge dangling clock earrings she wanted were $25, out of her price range. "Will yah git 'em for me, kid, soon as this is over?"

"Sure, we'll run right over."

The guy, a stocky, smelly Cuban who said his name was Juan and who everybody called "Don Juan," entered from the right. Brandy made a face but she went right ahead and made herself comfortable on the mattress that had been laid out on the floor of the gas station. The action started with a close-up of her running her hand across Juan's naked ass. They were shooting it from two angles because, they said, they needed one version for soft core, like for cable TV, the other for video cassettes.

As she opened her mouth to take Juan's still limp prick, she turned to me and whispered, "You know, I came out here more to be warm than to act."

"Hey, bitch, you're gonna be real warm in a minute," the director yelled at her. "Now cut the crap 'n suck that dick."

She seemed so much like me, so plain, so stupid, so honest, I suddenly felt sorry for her. I even felt sorry for Don Juan, not being able to get it up, and then I even began to feel sorry for myself. I liked fucking in private better than this. This was somehow taking being a whore too far. I decided I didn't want to do any more movies but that I would give them their money's worth.

"Okay, kid, let her suck both of yah."

I knelt down next to Don Juan and she struggled trying to get both of our cocks in her mouth at the same time, my hard one and Don's limp one. She worked one, then the other, then finally took them both. I had been told not to touch Don Juan, that this was a strictly straight video and men don't touch each other. I was glad about that because Juan was sweaty and too hairy for my taste. I looked up at the ceiling while Brandy went at it. One cameraman was shooting from the rear, the other aiming right at our dicks, getting every stroke as she went back and forth, then together. I wasn't getting off on this at all. I closed my eyes and thought about Kenny.

"...Okay, Juan you first."

Shit, I thought, I wanted to go first. Why didn't they let me fuck her pussy first, then it would have been over with and I could have collected my $200 and gone home. I straddled her head and began plowing into her mouth while Don fucked her cunt. I kept thinking about Kenny.

This scene seemed to go on for hours. My cock was really beginning to hurt. She tried her best but Juan was throwing it into her so hard, trying to get it hard, she'd slip and bite me. The cameramen were all over us. I began to really sweat and I hate to sweat. Then I felt myself going soft. I couldn't lose my hardon, not now. I kept thinking about Kenny and stroked it and suddenly I started to come. She gagged, tried to pull away, I grabbed for it, held it high, and came all over her face. One camera was on it and they were all cheering me.

"Great shot, kid. What a fuckin' load!"

After I climbed off of her and headed for the john, Juan just kept on. Poor Brandy just lay there with my juice all over her face. When I walked back into the garage, somebody had given her a towel and she was wiping her face. Her makeup was getting smeared all over and she looked like the slut I suppose she was. Juan just kept on. I couldn't believe it. Finally, the director yelled cut and we took a break.

"...You ready?" he asked me.

"Ready? I came. What more do you want?"

"You gotta fuck her, kid."

"No, man. Not for a million dollars." I didn't care if it ended my porn career.

I'd already made up my mind that wasn't something I wanted to do.

*

"I can't believe you did that!" Kenny screamed when I met him at the coffee shop off Sunset near Vine and told him I'd signed with Van and made a video, all in one day.

"When you're hot you're hot."

"Look, kid, porno's no good. And Van's dangerous. He'll book you into the worst scenes. A kid like you, you'll get the worst fuckin' scenes he can come up with."

"But you told him about me."

"Sure I did. But I didn't think you'd go for it. I get a finder's fee for every kid I send up there. But you didn't have to agree to workin' for him, much less a porno! Shit!" He shook his head angrily. "Look, I thought you'd just go up there and then run like crazy. Once he's into you, he wouldn't budge. No, Van's gotta have it all. And now he's got it."

"I can quit any time I want. I walked off the set. I don't want to do any more porno."

"Now that you're with Van you'd better not pull any more shit like that. You wouldn't be able to get shit in this town if you fucked him over. No, you're on your way, all right. Where to, I fuckin' don't know, but you're on your way."

I wanted Kenny to be jealous. Not mad about Van, just jealous that I was having sex all the time with everybody but him. Instead, he was mad at not getting a piece of the action. And, damn him, he looked better than I'd seen him in a long time. He'd dried out and was just sipping black coffee. Still, I knew it was only a matter of time before he'd start with the coke again. That's why I never started, because I knew I wouldn't be able to stop. "Just a joint now and then," I would tell everybody. But now it was Kenny's joint I was thinking about. When I was with him, it was hard to think about the business, about anything else. It had been so long. I could almost taste it.

"...You want to come back to my place?" I asked him as we left the coffee shop.

"Nah, kid, I gotta meet a bus. You know how it is."

Nodding, I stood there feeling like an idiot, not knowing what to say.

From the LP "I Remember You"/Sung by Joe Skinner/Side 1, Cut 4,
"Unforgettable:" "Unforgettable / That's what you are / Unforgettable /
Though near or far / Like a song of love that clings to me / How thoughts
of you do things to me / Never before has someone been more / Unforget-
table."

"Now that you're a porn star..." Van said over the phone.

"What?" I interrupted.

"Well, you did a couple of 'em and even if you never make any more - "

"I won't." He was still smarting from my walk-out. He hadn't called me in four days. I was getting desperate. I missed the business Kenny threw my way.

"Well, even if you don't, now you're a star, at least as far as the Star Fucker's concerned."

"The who?"

"I call him the Star Fucker. He's somebody in the music business I think. I don't know much about him really, 'cept he only wants guys that have been in pornos. And real studs. No sissies. Guys with big dicks that can always get it up. Guys with a history. Makes 'im feel safe, he says. Like, 'I got the goods on you, kid.'"

He was silent for a minute, waiting for me to say something but I didn't have anything to say.

"Yeah, the guy pays big bucks to have a porn stud fuck him."

"A stud? Me, a stud?"

"Well, you've the dick for it, kid."

"Yeah, and I sure don't have any trouble gettin' it up, unlike others I've seen that say they're studs, but I'm just a kid."

Just a kid but I learn quickly. Since I'd been in L.A., I learned a lot can depend on a little. After not having had much sex except with myself, suddenly sex was all there was. I just had to stand on the street corner and in a few minutes it would start again. In the beginning, it was a high more incredible, I was sure, than any fuckin' drug. I didn't need drugs. I'd seen so many kids hung up on drugs, I didn't want that. Me, I'd been set free by sex. The men became faceless. I just remembered cocks. And I learned what turned their little peckers on. I wasn't like the rest of the boys, in a hurry to get it over with so they could buy more crack. I even played hard to get, willing yet not so willing. I teased 'em. Teased 'em into wanting more. Yeah, a lot can depend on a little.

"Well, shit, where do I have to go?" I finally asked him.

"Way out almost to the beach. And allow youself plenty of time. Shit, I wish you had a fuckin' car."

"So do I. But hell, even if I could afford it, I couldn't drive it worth shit -"

"What?"

"Oh, never mind. I can handle a tractor on a field but I'm trouble behind the wheel of a car, man, that's all."

"Well, whatever," he said. I could hear the second line cutting in. He was busy all right, just not booking me. Till now. "Well, just give yourself plenty of time."

*

I didn't follow the Catman's advice. Sometimes I lose track of time and when I finally got my shit together and caught a cab we got stuck in a jam on the freeway. The driver swore we'd make better time on the freeway than just going out Sunset and we ended up waiting for 45 minutes, with the driver going on and on about his addiction to Ex-lax. Finally, I got out of the cab, walked down to the street and hitched a ride. I was at least an hour late. It was a place called the Lonely Sands Motel. I found the room right away. Just like Van said it would be, a sea green 1967 Chevy Malibu convertible was parked in front of the door. I knocked but there was no answer. I tried the door, it opened. It was late afternoon on a Sunday and the smog hadn't lifted all day so it was dull and gray, and I stepped into a dull, gray room. The spread had been pulled off the double bed and lying on the white sheets was a dude, on his stomach, nude. I stepped into the room and closed the door behind me. What struck me right off was the guy's back. I've seen naked backs but this was right out of the magazines. Like he was modelling for Calvin Klein. And then the ass. Absolutely perfect. More muscular looking than mine and very white against the deeply tanned rest of him. His left arm stretched across the bed and hung over the side. A bottle of Jack Daniels lay on the floor, nearly empty. He looked for all the world like he was dead but I figured he just passed out from drinking. It was my fault. If I'd been on time, he wouldn't have drunk so much and we'd be finished by now. I cleared my throat over and over, louder and louder, stepping closer and closer.

"Hey, man," I said finally, shaking his shoulder. He didn't come to. I looked around the room. There was a pair of tattered button-fly jeans hanging over a chair. I checked 'em out. No wallet, just a roll of cash, maybe $200, and car keys on a silver skull 'n' crossbones ring. I stuffed all of it back into the pockets of the jeans. There was a pair of black cowboy boots, very expensive ones, socks, and a smooth black silk shirt just thrown on the floor. Another bottle of bourbon and a liter of Coke sat on the bureau with a bucket of ice and some glasses, next to a pair of gold-rimmed Ray-Ban aviator sunglasses. I poured myself a Coke and sat on the edge of the bed. I waited.

I finally turned on the TV, real low, and watched a couple of movies. The end of one and the beginning of another. I'd seen them both before but I enjoyed 'em again coming up with the dialogue before the actors even got it out of their mouths.

Finally, the Star Fucker groaned and rolled over. The front view was even better than the back. His face reminded me of my hero, Randy Travis. And so did his torso. His legs were thin, a bit hairy, but his stomach was smooth, with a nice tuft of dark pubic hair. The cock, thick with a small head, hung to the left, with nice pink hairy balls. I leaned back between his legs and took his cock in my hand. I stroked it several times until he began groaning. Slowly he opened his eyes, then began blinking wildly. "What the?" he said, lifting himself up on his elbows.

I didn't say anything, just took the head of his cock between my lips and began sucking.

He looked at his watch. "How long you been here?"

"Coupla hours I guess. I'm not good with time."

He collapsed back on the bed. "Shit, shit, shit," he said, over and over.

Finally, he pushed me away. "Hey, I gotta get goin', kid. I'm late already."

"I'm the one who was late. I'm really sorry but the cab got stuck in traffic."

"Cab?"

"Yeah. I don't have a car."

"No fuckin' car in L.A.? What are you, nuts?" he asked, standing up.

When he stood up he was enough to take your breath away but I was able to mumble, "Yeah, I guess I am nuts." I wanted him in the worst way.

Suddenly he lurched forward, then dropped right back down on the bed again. "My head! Shit!"

I leaned against his body. I smelled an expensive cologne I couldn't place. I wanted to start licking his body and never stop. "I'm sorry I was late. It's all my fault." I kissed his shoulder.

"Yeah, yeah, it's all your fuckin' fault." He looked me in the eyes for the first time. "Hey, you're a beautiful little kid, ya know that?"

I blushed.

"Yeah, let me look at you." He took me by the shoulders and held me out as if he was judging me for a contest. "Yeah, you're hot."

"Thanks."

"But I can't believe Van sent you. You're just a fuckin' kid. I bet you're not even 18."

"I am. I've always looked young for my age."

"Well, if Van sent you you must have somethin'. What is it?" He chuckled. "I bet I can guess." His hand dropped to my crotch. He groped me hard. "God, would I love that! But," he said, rising from the bed again, "no time now. I've gotta get back."

He tried to walk but dropped back down on the bed, holding his head. "Christ, my head's killin' me."

"You'll feel better if you take a shower. I'll help you."

...He stayed in the bathroom for ten minutes. Finally he came out drying his hair with a towel. I was watching TV again. "You still here?" he asked with a chuckle.

His cock was semi-hard and I wanted to reach up and suck it again but I just sat there on the edge of the bed, waiting for him. He saw where my eyes were and brought the towel to it, stretching it, then drying the balls. It was a beauty, all right. Just as good as Kenny's. It was my fault, I was late.

He dropped the towel on the floor and picked up his jeans. After he tugged them on, he reached in the pocket and found his money roll. "You know, I can't figure it - "

"Figure what?"

"You find me in a drunken stupor and you don't steal my money or my car. No, you just wait for me to wake up! And then all you want to do is play. You can't have been in Hollywood very long - or the world for that matter!"

"No, I'm just a country boy."

"Oh, which country?"

"Ohio."

He laughed. "Ohio, shit! I'm from Alabama. Now that's country!"

...He said he'd drop me off on Melrose about a block from my little efficiency. He was a fast driver. Lots of weaving. The green buttons glowed on the Alpine car phone but it wasn't ringing. Supertramp was blarring on the stereo: "It's just a heart breaking / I should have known that it would let me down / It's just a mind aching / I used to dream about this town."

"Like that song?"

"No. I like Randy Travis, if you got any of his, like '8 X 10'."

He chuckled. "No, sorry, no country. How 'bout this," he said, pulling out Supertramp and slipping in another cassette. "It's brand new."

The song "Unforgettable" came on. "Nat King Cole," I said.

"Shit, no. One of the newer guys. White guy."

"But he's got soul," I said. "He almost sounds black."

I listened for a few minutes and then said, "Yeah, you can tell he's got soul. Randy Travis has soul, too. That's why I like him."
. He chuckled again and turned up the volume.

*

"...What the fuck did you do to the Star Fucker?" Van yelled into the phone.

"I was late."

"Late, shit! You should be late every time! He's never wanted to see anybody more than once, but he wants to see you again. You! I can't fuckin' believe it."

"I can't either."

"Look, it's for tomorrow night. And get this, he'll pick you up at the corner of Melrose and La Brea at 10 sharp. He says, 'Tell him not to be late.'"

"I won't. I'm never gonna be late again."

*

I was early. I pretended like I was waiting for the bus in case the cops drove by. Guys cruised me but I paid no attention. I could've made a hundred just waiting for my date.

"...Glad you could make it," he said. He had a baseball cap with "Sox" on it and his Ray-Bans. Sunglasses in the dark, I thought.

"Glad you invited me." "Unforgettable" was playing on the stereo again. "I'm beginning to like that song."

"Me, too," he said, his hand dropping to my thigh. "Come over here."

I edged closer and leaned against him.

"You're a strange one, you know," he said.

"So are you."

...He didn't waste any time. He turned on Vine and went a block and a half, pulling in at the Econo Lodge. He handed me a fifty. "Rent us a room, okay?"

I got the key and walked to the room while he followed in the car.

I opened the door to the room and held it open for him. He looked both ways before he got out of the Chevy, then came in. Closing the door behind him, he held out his arms. "I'll bet you're a good kisser."

"Not usually." I suddenly realized I'd never kissed a trick. I'd never even kissed Kenny. But I wanted to kiss this guy, whoever he was. I wanted to kiss every part of him.

It was a movie star kiss all right. Like Monty Clift and Liz Taylor in "A Place in the Sun." I didn't care who he was, I wanted to eat him up.

"...Wait, wait," he pleaded when I dropped to my knees in front of him and started to unzip his pants. He pulled me up by the shoulders like he did the last time and held me, staring at me. "Shit, you are a pretty one."

And then he kissed me again. His hands were all over my body, pressing me against him. I ran my hands up and down his back, remembering how gorgeous it was. I smelled the liquor on his breath but I didn't mind. In fact, I was practically getting high from it as he shoved his tongue between my teeth, then started eating my chin, my cheeks, my ears, then my nose. All I wanted to do was eat him up but he was eating me. "Hmmm, you taste so good," he cried and kept at it, pulling my shirt out of my jeans and unbuttoning it, then lowering it off of me. His mouth slid down my neck and onto my shoulders, sucking, biting, kissing, licking. I got a fierce hard-on and rubbed it against him. "Oh, yeah," he cried.

I fell to my knees again, to escape him but also to work on his crotch. I had left the zipper undone and I reached in and grabbed it. He let me this time and I took it all in one gulp, then pulled it out and worked on the balls. He was hard in no time and I blew him like that, on my knees in the fuckin' Econo Lodge on Vine Street. When he was close, I stood up and led him to the bed. Suddenly, he was putty in my hands. If he wanted a porno stud then he was gonna get a porno stud. I undressed him completely and then worked on his cock some more, bringing it back up and ready to pop. I rolled him over on his stomach. The buns, gleaming in the dim light, were as beautiful as I'd remembered. I couldn't imagine anybody having a nicer ass than that. My cock was so hard it jumped out of my pants as I pulled them down.

He looked behind him as I undressed. All he did was groan.

Sliding a lubed rubber on my dick, I mounted him and started sliding back and forth across his ass. He reached around and took my dick in his hand. "You're from a farm all right, a stud farm."

"You get what ya pay for," I chuckled, and let him guide it in.

...He couldn't get enough of it. He had to have it in every position he could think of, but it ended up with us sitting on the bed facing each other, his thighs over mine, my cock in him, holding each other. He moved it the way he wanted it and started kissing me again. I had no idea what it meant to be in love but at that moment I knew I'd gone into a different orbit. He came but kept on, going crazy with it. Finally, he had me pull out and he took the rubber off and sighed, "I hardly ever suck cock but this is somethin' else." He kissed it and then began sucking. He wasn't good at it but he was enjoying himself so I just closed my eyes and held onto his shoulders. When I came he was so happy he kissed me again.

After I took a shower and came back into the bedroom, he was still lying there, still nude, his eyes shut. I dropped down on the bed and kissed his navel.

"I've been thinking," he said, slowly, deliberately.

"Yeah.?"

"I want you to come back to the house with me."

"You do?"

"I know I shouldn't but I just have these great vibes. I can't explain it. I've only felt like this once or twice before and it was always somewhere else, like Mexico or Rio." He stroked my hair. "It's like I know I'm gonna want you tomorrow morning before I go to the studio and you won't be there and -"

"The studio?"

"Yeah, I'm working at Disney and I've gotta get up at six every morning. They spend an hour every day on my makeup and all I do is sit around all day. It's boring as hell, but it's almost over."

Disney? I thought Van had said this guy was in the music business. Now I find he's a Mickey Mouse. I started to chuckle.

"What's so funny?"

"Nothin'. Just me and Mickey Mouse! I never thought I'd be going to bed with Mickey Mouse!"

"Hey," he said, chuckling, "they make more than cartoons there now, you know. This thing we're doing is a sci-fi piece of shit. I play an alien for chrissakes!"

"Best looking alien I've ever seen," I said, hugging him.

"I'll call Van and tell him you're on special assignment and can't be reached."

And he picked up the phone and did just that. I would have loved to have seen the look on Van's fat face while he was listening to it.

It was two in the morning when we got in the old Chevy and soon he was speeding up into the foothills, on Mulholland Drive. We stopped at a gate almost hidden by the trees and he slipped a card into a slot and suddenly we were passing through the brick walled entrance, past a tiled fountain and into a double garage. From what I could see in the darkness, this was something right out of the movies.

"It's an old house," he said. "Built in 1928. I bought it a couple of years ago but this is the first time I've actually lived here for any length of time. But it's lonely, just me and the maid."

I realized I still didn't have a clue as to who this guy was. Here I was in a hilltop house with somebody who was playing an alien in a Disney movie and as many movies as I'd watched in my life I couldn't place him. "Have you been in any other movies?"

"Only one. It bombed. But it's become what they call a cult

classic."

No help there. We went into the house. Every room was on a different level and the view from every room was out of this world. From the living room I could see the flats, from downtown to the Ocean.

"This is the loggia," he said, leading me out onto a wooden balcony. I got dizzy looking out over what he called Cahuenga Pass. I felt I was suspended in space. He led me down the stairs to where the master bedroom was, then the guest bedroom below it, all hanging on to the side of the cliff. More steps down led to a tiny garden and when he flicked on more lights I could see it was full of spine-covered prickly pears and there was a hottub almost hidden in all the greenery. "Wanna soak?" he asked.

Struck dumb by all of it, I didn't even answer, I just started taking off my clothes.

Soon we were in the tub and he was kissing me again like before and I never wanted the night to end.

From the LP "I Remember You"/Sung by Joe Skinner/Side 1, Cut 5, "I Could Get Used to This:" "...Imagine my surprise when I found you / Darling, I have nursed this lonely heart so long / It's hard to let go and trust that we belong / I could get used to this / Having you to hold me through the night / I could get used to this..."

"It's my housekeeper Matty's day off," he whispered, "so you'll be alone all day. I'll be back by seven. If you need anything, the number in my trailer at the studio's written next to the phone in the kitchen."

I rubbed my eyes and looked at the clock on his nightstand. It wasn't even seven a.m. He kissed the top of my head and was gone. For a long while I lay there in the huge bed trying to fit all the pieces together. The afternoon at the beach, last night. Now.

I looked around the room. It was an ordinary bedroom, I decided, in an extraordinary house. Everything was beige, the walls, the rug, the draperies, the satin sheets on the bed. But it was the mirrors that fascinated me. He loved watching us together. He liked it best on his knees, his elbows digging into the bed, watching the action in the mirror that filled the entire wall alongside the bed. "Better than any video, eh, kid?" he said several times. Since my only experience with sex videos was being in two of them, I didn't even try to answer.

I hugged the pillows and began to fuck them the way I had fucked him, after we'd blown each other in the hot tub. I was getting off on how I fucked him in his bed until he couldn't take it any more and how I fell asleep holding onto his arm, afraid he might disappear if I didn't.

After I came, I tried to go back to sleep but I couldn't. I was too excited to sleep.

My first day on the hilltop was one of discovery. It was an even more marvelous place in the daytime than it had been at night. As I stepped out the front door, I smelled the flowers and felt the tingle of the mix of dew and warm sunshine. What a day, I thought. Then I remembered that it was like this every day in California but I was feeling it as if it were the first time. I prowled around the house like a burglar, one room to the next until I found what I was looking for, just by accident. It was a record album, one of many stacked by the wall in the living room that had a TV and every kind of electronic gadget you could imagine. "The Skins, 1976" was the name of it and on the back cover was a picture of the group. In the middle of the line of four guys with no shirts on and close-cropped hair was the man I'd just spent the night with. Only now he had long hair almost down to his shoulders and a little mustache. He was Joe Skinner. I said the name over and over again. I didn't know much about rock 'n' roll, being a country fan, but I had heard of the group. They were big in the late '70s and early '80s. Two of the guys eventually OD'd and they stopped recording. That was all I knew. I sifted through the records and the tapes. There were maybe five of the Skins, each with a year after their name, and then I found the tape I was looking for. Joe was alone on the cover, wearing his "Sox" baseball cap and he had his legs stretched out real sexily. "Joe Skinner Sings Songs of Love, I Remember You," it said on the cover. I wanted to kiss that fucking cover, he was so adorable. I bet millions of girls did kiss the fucking cover. I turned the box over and read the song titles. "Unforgettable" was there, all right. It was Joe singing that afternoon in the Chevy. I pulled the tape out of the box and slipped it into the player. I was prepared to like it. What happened was, I loved it. Right from the first song, I knew this guy had a voice that was almost as good as Randy Travis'. I couldn't believe it.

I had come to Hollywood because somebody on TV said Randy Travis was here and then somebody told me that he lived in Nashville with an older woman who was his manager. I began saving up to go to Nashville.

But now I was on a hilltop in Hollywood in Joe Skinner's house. It was like my grandpa used to say, "Ya take what God gives ya, kid."

As the music followed me from room to room I went back to Joe Skinner's bedroom. I pulled the drapes open and the room was filled with sunshine. I looked into the mirror again. I ran my hands over my body. All I knew was that I suddenly really loved looking at myself. Incredible as it seemed, a handsome rock star loved the way I made him feel. He was somebody that could order up anybody he wanted but he'd ask me to stay. But I didn't look like my own idea of what a stud was. Oh, I had a thick, long dick all right but I was just a kid. A short little kid. But then I remembered how Joe got off on it and how great it felt being up his ass and deep down his throat. I must be able to do something right. What I saw in the mirror was a different person than I knew me to be. And last night I had seen a different man than the public, especially the screaming teenage girls who were his fans, knew to be Joe Skinner. Or maybe mirrors have a way of distorting things, that we are nothing more than reflections, reflections of a crazy, mixed up world where so many people think what we were doing is bad, so bad that they're always trying to take away the mirrors and shatter them.

And now, listening to Joe singing, I started to sway back and forth with the melody. And the music worked its magic. The song was "I Could Get Used to This." I jacked off again to my own reflection and could hardly wait until seven o'clock.

*

The limo pulled up the drive a few minutes after seven. I watched from the window as he stepped from the car, said something to the driver, and crossed the patio. Seeing him again after 12 hours alone, I fell in love with him all over again. He was so cool. I shivered just thinking he was coming home to me. I was glad I'd taken a shower, splashed on his cologne and put on a pair of shorts I'd found in his closet that, if I pulled 'em tight enough, sort of fit me.

"Hi, Joe," I said as he was coming through the door.

He smiled. "Now you know, eh?"

"Hell, I've had all day to find out."

"Okay," he said and he held me in his arms. "Unforgettable" started playing again on the stereo. It seemed so incredible to have the man who was singing actually holding me in his arms.

"I've been listening to it all day."

"God, you must be bored out of your mind with it."

"No, it's all I ever want to hear."

He kissed me on the tip of my nose. "You always know the right thing to say. How do you do it?"

"Just honest, I guess."

"That's what I like about you, kid." He kissed me hard on the mouth and then we went to the hot tub and took turns blowing each other. Eventually, we made it to the bedroom.

He liked to watch me coming toward him naked. I would start at the bathroom and work my way across the room and to the bed, taking the long way, stopping in front of the big mirror and doing a little posing into it, my erection growing stronger by the minute. I would step over to the bed and he'd be lying there on his stomach, propped up with his elbows and I'd stand in front of him with my hands on my hips, my cock swaying before his eyes. I'd step closer and closer, my cock caressing his cheeks, his lips, his eyes. He'd run his hands up and down my thighs and try to catch the tip of my cock with his lips. Eventually, he'd have it in his mouth and I'd start shoving it, gently, deep into his throat. He'd look to the side so he could watch in the other mirror behind the headboard.

"...Do you want to stay?" he asked after three hours of sex, with a break for some beer and pizza that he'd had delivered from the Pizza Kitchen on La Cienega ("Best in town," he said, and he ordered it with Peking duck topping).

"Sure. Who wouldn't," I said, rubbing his chest.

"Okay. I want to hire you -"

"Hire me?"

"You are in business, as I recall."

"Oh, yeah. I guess so. Well, now I guess I'm retired."

"Oh, really?"

"Yeah, retired at the ripe old age of 18." I laid back and closed my eyes.

"So, what kind of pension is suitable for an 18-year-old?" He had his hand on my cock again.

"I dunno. Just leave a little something on the nightstand when you leave in the morning. I'll get by."

*

Earlier, he'd noticed I was wearing his shorts, before he peeled them off as we got in the hot tub, and he asked me if I wanted to go back to my little room and get my things. I said yes. So the next day after the limo took him to the studio he had the driver, Harold, come back and take me to the apartment. Joe had left two hundred dollar bills on the nightstand that morning so I paid the landlady what I owed and Harold helped me lug my things to the car. The old woman stood at the door to her apartment watching us put my suitcases in the trunk. I don't think she could believe this little kid was moving from her crappy old efficiency to a white stretch Lincoln limo; so after everything was packed I went up to her and said, "You should see the house!" Then I winked. She shook her head and slammed the door in my face.

Joe called Matty "Old Pruneface" behind her back but he said he loved her. She had been his maid ever since he bought the house and he could trust her. He told her I was his nephew from Ohio and would be staying in the guest room for a week or two. So when I came into the house with my old suitcases with Ohio State stickers on them and my little TV, she must have assumed that was the truth. I didn't tell her they were my father's old suitcases. (I had always wondered about it; why my father had to go to college to become a farmer. All I ever did on the farm was shovel shit and mend fences. He said, "You gotta go to college in order to learn to do anything these days." I wondered if I had to go to college to have sex correctly, that maybe going to college would have made my fantasies of having sex with another boy go away and I would think about girls from then on.)

"You Mr. Skinner's sister's boy?"

"Yeah, I guess you could say that," I replied, figuring Joe must have had a sister or a brother somewhere since I was his nephew.

"From Ohio?"

"Well, no that's where I go to school. We're all from Alabama, though, you know." I tried a Southern drawl but I don't think she bought it.

She nodded. "You flunk out?"

"I guess you could say that."

She just shook her head and went on making the apple pie we were going to have for dessert that night. ("Apple's Mr. Skinner's favorite," she said. "Mine, too," I answered. I felt very all-American right then, almost collegiate.)

When Joe came home, he looked at my belongings and shook his head. "I think you could use some new things."

"What for, I never go anywhere?"

"Well, you might and this stuff looks like you got it at a rummage sale."

"I did. My dad never bought anything new if he could help it. Even my mother had been divorced twice. It was like the song from

'Funny Girl,' 'Second Hand Rose.'"

It was decided. The next day, Harold took me shopping. We went to Ralph Lauren on Rodeo Drive. Joe had said I could buy anything I wanted but when I got to the store the clerk said that Joe had phoned and given him a list. All I had to do was pick out which colors I wanted and try everything on.

When Joe got home, I modelled every outfit. I discovered that clothes can be very sexual. That they can do more than just reveal a big basket. Good clothes, expensive clothes, tailored ones, made me look like Joe wanted me to look. I looked in the mirror and didn't even know the person. It didn't look like me but it was somebody Joe liked. A lot.

"These are great," I said. "Like I told you, I've never worn anything that hadn't been damaged before I put it on."

"You'll never wear damaged goods again."

I collapsed on the bed next to him. "But I'm damaged goods, Joe. That's the way I feel, like I shouldn't be here with you. I don't belong."

He kissed me. "Look, kid, anything you've done, well, it was practice. Practice for now. If you hadn't done all that, well, you wouldn't be here now."

And I knew he was right. And I dug him all the more.

Later that night, after we had the dinner Matty left, he poured us brandies. He swirled it around in the big glass and then drank some of it. I tried it but didn't care for it. I decided I'd like it better if it were on his cock, so I poured some of it there so I could lick it off. "Whoa," he said, as I dribbled some on his crotch. I licked and sucked him, now loving the taste of brandy and sweat and precum, until he was going wild, pushing my head down into it, forcing it deep inside my throat, thrusting it deeper and deeper, then waiting for me, then again and again until he came. It was the first time he'd come in my mouth. It was warm and sticky and just kept coming. He usually came while I was fucking him, but he said he couldn't help himself.

Cum oozing from the sides of my mouth and onto my chin, he pulled me on top of him and licked my face clean. His hand found my cock and knew I was ready. He took his own snifter and poured brandy all over my cock and started in, but I knew what he wanted. I pulled away, got a rubber and when I walked back to the bed he asked for it. As he began sliding it on, he kissed my balls. When he had rolled it all the way on, he held it in his hand, looked up into my eyes and sighed, "Hmmm, I could get used to this."

And I was sure the smile on my face was the biggest one I'd ever had in my whole life.

From the LP "I Remember You"/Sung by Joe Skinner/Side 2, Cut 1, "What a Difference A Day Makes:" "...Twenty four little hours...My yesterdays used to be blue, dear / Today I'm a part of you, dear / Lord, what a difference a day makes / There's a rainbow before me / Skies above me can be stormy / Since that moment of bliss / That thrilling kiss / It's heaven when you find romance on your menu / What a difference a day makes / And the difference is you."

I made it a point to get up in the morning, slip into my new silk robe, and fix a pot of coffee and put out some of Matty's homemade cinnamon rolls for him. I also put "I Remember You" on the stereo, filling the house with his husky voice. He hated it. "I can't stand it!" he'd scream. "Turn that fuckin' thing off!"

"But I love it," I'd say, ignoring him as one of my favorites, "Easy to Love," came on while he was finishing his first cup of coffee. "That song sounds so familiar," I said.

"It should. It's by Cole Porter."

"It's odd. Certain things I can remember now but don't know why. As if it happened in some other life."

"That was another life. Whatever went before, it was another life. This is your life now."

I wanted to believe him but something told me, taking everything into account, I was only passing through. But I was determined to make the most of it. When Harold drove up the drive and tooted the horn, Joe jumped up and was gone, but not before he kissed me. He always kissed me goodbye.

*

That night when he came home he was furious. He threw the *National Enquirer* across the room and poured himself a strong Jack Daniels. He hadn't drunk anything stronger than beer or wine since I had moved in. He gulped it down like my grandpa and my pa used to, then poured another. It was as if he was slowly turning into a wild animal, like that movie "Dr. Jekyll and Mr. Hyde."

I went to him, tried to stop him, but it was like he'd gone insane.

He shoved the newspaper in my face. I stared at it. His picture was on the front page and I tried to read the headline as best I could.

"Read it!" he screamed. "Fuckers!"

I stood there scanning the type of the article on the inside. I started to mumble.

"Well?"

"I can't make much out of it."

"Shit, man, you mean you fuckin' can't read?"

"I can read, it's just that it gets mixed up sometimes. Backwards sometimes. I can't explain it."

"Oh my God! Just what I need, a fuckin' mental cripple! My sister was a mental cripple. Shit-" Suddenly he stopped. It was as if a light went on in his head. "What am I saying? What am I saying to you?"

He took me in his arms and shook me. I was afraid of him for the first time. His eyes were like fire, staring right into mine. He started to cry. But he kept shaking me. Harder and harder. I couldn't lift my arms to defend myself. All I could do was finally pull myself free. I ran out of the living room, down the steps to my room. I sat on the bed, terrified of what might come next. I had let him down. He'd found out my secret. They always found out my secret. In the end, everyone knew. I wanted to hide, to run away but I couldn't. I knew the front gate was locked and the only way out would have been off the balcony and down the rocks. I didn't move. I just sat on the edge of the bed the way I did back home when my father would start in after my mother died when I was nine: "They say you're sick in the head," he'd yell. "They're not tellin' me anything's wrong with my kid. No, sir!" And he would smash the dishes and then slam the door behind him. When I'd hear him get in the pick-up to drive into town, I knew it was safe to turn on the TV and watch my movies. Later, when I saved up, I bought my own TV, a little black and white one, and then I didn't ever have to go downstairs.

I could hear Joe on the steps, then he stood in the doorway. The sun was setting behind him and it made him look like Christ rising from the grave. "I'm sorry," he mumbled.

This wasn't my father. This wasn't anybody I'd ever known. Nobody'd ever said they were sorry before.

I started to cry. Joe came into the room, put his arms around me and hugged me. I must have sobbed for a good five minutes.

"You know," he said, finally, "now my sister can read better than I can. She teaches school in Alabama, for chrissakes! My father got the best people in the country working on it and I learned all about it. You can be cured." He kissed the top of my head. "I shouldn't have said what I did."

I didn't say anything, I just hugged him harder than I had ever hugged anybody in my entire life.

They say you can get used to anything but I never did. I never got used to being made a fool of.

I stood up in class.

"It's your turn," the teacher, Mrs. Snodgrass, said.

"But I can't."

"It's time you did."

"I can't."

"You really should try harder."

"But sometimes I see things backwards."

And as the kids howled with laughter, I sat down again and wanted to die.

When I got home, I told my father, "I hate school."

"But the teachers say you're smart. I just don't understand it."

"I don't either."

"I had one of those teachers tell me it's sometimes caused by a head injury, then I got to thinking, you used to bang your head against the wall. We couldn't stop you. Just bang bang bang."

"Oh, please, pa."

"Shit, boy, if you can't read you're no better than apes in a zoo."

And the last thing he ever said to me was when he dropped me off at the bus station: "I won't be writing you. No point, is there?"

He pulled our pants away and had me slide between his thighs and he guided it into his ass. He just wanted me to be in him, and to hold him, and so did I. He gently wiped away my tears and we kissed each other. As I slowly fucked his ass, he told me he was tired so I jacked him off. "Please, don't cum inside of me," he moaned, and I didn't. I let my cock slide out and then I came on his chest.

Later, after we'd returned to the living room, I asked, "...What was it that got you so upset?"

"They've dug up some cunt that says she was with Paul and me the night he died. I'm convinced they can find somebody that'll say anything for a price."

"Do you know her?"

"Hardly! Shit, if I could remember a tenth of the cunts I fucked on the road it'd be amazing. They get thrown at you every night. It's just a matter of which one gets there first." He took the paper and shoved it in my face again. "Now, would you remember somebody that looked like that?"

"No, but that's not a fair question. I'm not into cunts."

"Oh, yeah," he chuckled. "Well, I was into 'em for a long time and where did it get me?"

"All over the 'Enquirer' it looks like. But it's a great shot of you." They had used a picture of him on stage, at the height of their popularity. I decided he looked even better now, especially reflected in the mirrors of his bedroom, bouncing up and down on my cock.

"I'm gonna sue, that's what I'm gonna do." He took up the paper and read the article out loud. The bitch claimed that five years ago, when they were appearing in Indianapolis, she had met Paul and was in his hotel room after a show. Her story was that Joe came to the room, gave them drugs and partied with them, then left around 3 a.m. Before dawn, Paul was dead from an overdose. The girl left the hotel room and never reported her participation in the incident. Until now.

"Why now?" I asked when he was finished.

"Fuck, how should I know! Maybe with the album out it occurred to her that I'd want her story, whatever bullshit it is, stopped. That I'd pay to have it stopped. But I won't pay blackmail. Benny told me somebody had called but I told him there was nothing to it."

"Benny?"

"Benny Kaplan discovered us when we were in school in Athens over ten years ago. He was like a father to us. He still handles all my business." He looked at me calculatedly. "Benny doesn't approve, you know."

"Approve of what?"

"When I called him today about this trash in the paper, I told him I had a house guest. He said he wanted to meet you."

"Okay."

"Haha! Wait'll he does, man. Wait'll be does! But I'm not rushing it. He thinks I've gone crazy again. I told him you were helping me with my memoirs. I told him I needed somebody to help me get everything down so I could go public with the whole thing. If they're still interested, shit, they should know the truth."

"So that's why I'm here, to help you with your book?" I rubbed his crotch.

"Insane, isn't it? You haven't known me a week but you're helping me with the story of my life!" He took me in his arms again and hugged me. "Well, you're a part of it now, you might as well help with it."

"Shit, I can't even read. What good am I?"

"Your mind, it's like a fuckin' tape recorder. I've heard you, everything you ever heard on TV or the radio you've got memorized. "

Not quite. I'd memorized bits of dialogue. Words came at me like riddles, most of the time. People were like concrete to me, their faces, gestures, clothing, eyes, odors, voices. I didn't remember their names most of the time, unless I worked at it. Stars names were easiest. I heard them, knew them. I didn't have to read them.

"You can just listen while I talk and then you can put it all down. We'll teach you to put it all down."

"Like in 'Auntie Mame' when Mame tells Patrick to write down every word he doesn't know - "

"See, there you go again!"

"But how can I put it down? If you can't read, you can't write."

"If my sister can do it, you can do it. Trust me."

"I do." And I reached down to find he had a hardon again. At least there was something I could do for him.

*

It seemed he suddenly had a cause besides going to the studio every day at seven and getting fucked every night. He remembered things best after he'd had a drink, "just one, to help with the tongue," he'd say. And I knew he meant that in more ways than one.

Once he said, "I got this feeling I don't have long, you know? Like, we're all dying, all the time. Every day." He seemed to be preoccupied by death. Always dying. He was dying of thirst.

Dying for a joint. Dying for my cock. He was always dying and it seemed like I had just started to live. I gave him my line from "Hell's Angels." He just shook his head.

"Yeah, life," he said once, "it teaches you to be cautious. You'll also learn to be more careful how you judge the rest of us."

"I don't judge you, Joe."

"That's what I love about you. You don't. I tell you I did all these things that might blow some people's minds or that I fucked a thousand cunts or whatever and you don't say anything. And you don't do anything, you're just here." He took me in his arms. "Just for me."

I kissed him. "Why you want me I don't know but as long as you do, I'm here."

"I want you because you're different. There's something special about you. And I don't mean just that big cock. I must have had a dozen guys come to that motel. They were zeros, every one of them. Most of 'em couldn't even keep it up." He groped my crotch. "Hmmm, you're different all right. And I know if I got into trouble you'd be the one who'd help me out of it. I can feel that."

"Like a mother?"

"God, no. Not a mother. More like a brother. You know, I never had a brother, just a sister. I always wanted a brother. But you're better than a brother."

"Yeah, I'm legal. A brother'd be incest." I slipped out of my bikini and stroked my dick for him. It was hard again. Every time he looked at it, it got hard.

From the LP "I Remember You"/Sung by Joe Skinner/Side 2, Cut 2, "Impossible:" "...If they had ever told me | How sweet a kiss could be | I would have said, impossible | Impossible for me | And if they said I'd find you | Beyond the rainbow's end | I would have said, impossible | Impossible, my friend | To dream about what might have been is strange enough for me | But now it seems I'm living in a dream too beautiful to be | ...Now it seems nothing is impossible..."

The evening was our time for remembrances. When Matty didn't come to the house and leave dinner, Joe would order Peking duck from Mr. Chow or New York steak from Trumps sent in. "Don't eat so fast. And little bites. Chew slowly," he'd say. It made him happy to see me polishing the manners my mother had taught me long ago. It seemed with Joe it was natural to be perfect, to do everything just like rich people do in the movies. It was as if we were in the movies.

If he didn't go to the studio, the morning was our time for new ideas. He'd wake up fresh, ready to work. I'd always look forward to the mornings, hoping that on days he had to go to the studio, he'd get really inspired and want to finish a story, then he'd let me ride along in the limo. We'd arrive at the lot, the big Disney lot in Burbank, where the white water tower has Mickey Mouse on it and all the bushes are made into little mouse sculptures. And we'd tool right through the gates, everybody tipping their hat to him, to the car, to Harold. Joe would get out and tell Harold to take me right home and put me to work.

On the way home, I would sit in the limo listening to one of his tapes, usually my favorite, "I Remember You," trying to figure out what made him so irresistible.

I couldn't put my finger on it but it was like someone on TV had said: "You can't describe what Joe Skinner has but he has it. He's like pornography, you can't describe it but you know it when you see it. It's that thing they've come to call charisma. His voice is charismatic. We know he can be that way in person, when he wants to, but his voice, always." Little did he know how much like pornography Joe was.

*

Joe arranged to have the "Professor" come every other day. That's what I called him. He was a tutor to people like me and Joe was paying him to give his nephew private lessons.

He started with the lyrics to Joe's songs on the new LP. "Uncomplicate the words," he said, but it was difficult for me. And it was boring; sometimes I wanted to throw up my hands and quit, but the Professor was very patient and when Joe arrived he'd give me a good report. I always suspected other men, always searched for clues, but the Professor was so dead-ahead straight he was comfortable. I could relax and concentrate. I was required to read the lyrics five times without a mistake before we went on to another song. "You must learn to pay attention," he kept saying.

"Why is it you can watch TV or mess around with that tractor for hours and hours, yet you can't read?" my pa used to ask.

I had no answer. What I considered real, teachers considered fantasy. What I considered fantasy, they considered real. Words came at me like a riddle, uninvited, boring.

My mother, before she died, went to the counselor at the school and said, "He can't be disabled. He's so well coordinated. Has been since he could walk. His problem is the teachers. They don't have time to spend with the kids anymore."

"Mom," I said, "it's not their fault."

"Well, it's not your fault and it's not my fault. I don't know whose fault it is, but it has to be somebody's fault."

"Can't something just happen without it being someone's fault? Mom, it's the way I am. Nobody's to blame."

"No. You're not the way you are. And somebody's to blame."

"I'm just slow."

"If you say that again I'll hit you right here. Somebody's got to knock some sense into you. If your father can't - "

"Here we go again," I said, standing up.

"Keep your mouth shut and sit down," she said.

"Look," the counselor said, "let's try to forget the past. William is bright enough. We'll see if we can find a teacher who can help."

"It's hopeless," I said, racing out of the room.

They never found a teacher who could help.

The Professor said he was going to use what he called the melody technique. "Melody is the ease at being what we are and doing what we do. It is the center of wholeness in a frog that makes it jump, in a lizard that makes it skitter, in a dog that makes it fetch. In humans, it makes them communicate with spoken and written symbols. Without melody, we move without direction. It unites reception and expression. When the body and the mind dance to melody there are no wallflowers."

"You mean flowerwalls."

"That's what you used to say. But no more."

"No more."

"If melody is involved, the eyes, ears and the rest of the body have to join in, and you block out the rest of the senses to bring everything in balance. You are marvelously coordinated so what we are doing is transferring your body-mind-brain melody to perceptual, semantic melody, your physical coordination for sensory coordination. It's the best kind of transfer."

Symbols were the hardest. "Look at those symbols, examine them from every angle, write them so you get to know them up close from every angle, build their 'melody of movement' in your body, then your mind. You'll seldom confuse them again." I began to feel comfortable with them. I would make guesses, "with strong clues woven by melody," the Professor said, and it would almost always equal certainty. "Almost equal" became the words we used as he kept making me practice. After I would write a sentence a few times, he would require me to write it again with my eyes closed. I continued to write it, one time eyes open, one time closed, until the rhythm of it took over. If I made a mistake, I would correct it in the next writing. If a sound or word showed up alone and lonely it began repeating itself as if it was looking for company. We put the music on and I wrote the lyrics down, dancing with them, getting them right more often than I got them wrong. My handwriting had always been terrible and it improved, improved so much that Joe could actually read the lyrics. The pages became love letters to him that I stuck everywhere so he could find them.

Joe had a computer delivered and put in his den. The Professor convinced him it was the perfect thing for me: "I've had boys that have had the same difficulty William has and they've gone on to be computer programmers. Their persistence, accuracy and speed at visual tasks such as keyboard work make them ideal."

"See," Joe said to me, "and you thought you were disabled, for chrissakes."

He started me on the games and finally I was actually writing sentences on the computer. The Professor would check my work when he visited. It was easy to correct the mistakes on the computer. Sometimes I'd have the TV on and type the dialogue from the movies as they were saying it. I had memorized bits of dialogue so that I could say them and feel important. Now I was doing the whole script. "You've learned to type in the bargain," the Professor teased me. "I want a bonus."

Before I met Joe the only bonus I could give him was between my legs, but now I found myself saying, "I'll have Joe take care of it." The Professor laughed.

Matty would have to bring my lunch into me; Joe would come home and have to drag me away from the computer. "I'm so proud of you," he'd say. And then I'd fuck him silly. He'd scream for me to stop and when I did, he'd beg me to continue. He was so happy I always had a hardon. "I guess if you're gonna have a stud around, get one who's 18," he'd say.

I started to say, If you're gonna have a sugar daddy, get one who's under thirty and a movie star, but I didn't.

*

"...That must have been wild," I told Benny. (Joe had said: "We had our attorneys, our agents and our manager. But Benny was like the fifth member of the group. His vote counted the same.")

"Yeah," he went on, lighting another cigarette. "I couldn't imagine a life when you didn't have to check the exits! Check security! Oh, but, it was a time when there were no reservations, no checking thoughts before you went to bed, you could just live. We'll never see those days again."

"No."

"But if I hadn't done that I would've been involved in entertainment, somehow. I love the idea of promoting, hustling, hyping. I like that kind of vaudeville, snake oil, extravaganza thing. Not only selling things but convincing 'em they need it. And when you've convinced them, they're just amazed that they ever lived without it."

I thought of saying, "Sorta like living with Joe Skinner," but I didn't.

"Yeah, the boys loved that life for a long time. All the booze, all the drugs, all the sex they could ever want. They were living everybody's fantasy about what it was supposed to be. But the truth is, they were just covering up; they weren't the Stones or Van Halen; they were just ordinary guys, really."

"Yeah, sure."

He smiled. "So what does Joe want to know?"

"Things you wouldn't tell him to his face."

"There's nothing I wouldn't tell Joe Skinner to his face."

"Well - "

"He can tell you all about it. I suppose he has. Those were long nights. I never thought he'd make it. He really wasn't cut out for it. He was just singing in the choir at school when we asked him to front the group. You see, in the old days, there was the orchestra or band or whatever and they had a singer. Sometimes a woman, sometimes a man. Sometimes both. You had to have a pretty face upfront. Same today. Joe made the group complete. We changed the name and went on the road. He wasn't much of a singer in those days, but good enough. Today, he's a great singer but he wants to do all these old things. That new album is a mistake."

"It's wonderful."

"You think so? See, I don't understand kids today. You can't even be 18 and you like it."

"I am 18, but I'm not your usual kid."

He laughed. "I can see that. But, still, you like the songs."

"The way he sings 'em, I like 'em. I like country music and the way he sings them, well, it's like that. Lots of feeling. It's different than rock 'n' roll."

"I'll give it that. It's different all right. I wish him well with it. I didn't like the contract we got with those Disney people. Their label's never had a hit. After two years, not a hit. You know what Pearson, he's the honcho over there, you know what he told me? 'So we lose $20 million, we've got $700 million!' That's the kind of people you're dealing with! Look, they've got Queen, right? Imagine, Joe Skinner and Queen! Paulie would have had a heart attack! Anyhow, we went to the party they threw for Queen's new album. They held it on the Queen Mary, for chrissakes! Anyhow, me and Joe go to this thing and there's Michael Eisner, who runs the whole damn studio, sitting between two loudspeakers blaring this Queen shit! Joe got a drink and all I got was a headache! And now he's making a movie for them besides!" He shook his head. "Did ya see the billboard on Sunset, kid?"

I shook my head; I hadn't.

"When you go back, take a look. Bigger than anyone else's. He looks great."

I made a note to tell Harold to drive by it.

"Yeah, Joe's coming back. I'm happy for him."

"Do you think he should come out?"

"Should what?"

"Come out, you know, tell everybody he likes men?"

"Why?"

"Why not?"

"Look, I know Joe. He used to say he likes to watch the wheels go round. Now, I interpret that as anything from watching peple have sex to looking at people walking down the street. But whatever he's into is nobody's business. It makes no difference what anybody does in the dark as long as they are consenting adults. I'll never change my philosophy on that. Never. And you'll never change Joe's. Look what happened in this town when Rock got it. A whole new wave of homophobia set in. No, you'll never convince us anybody should know what we do between the sheets."

I went to his small office in downtown L.A. because Joe decided I should meet him on his own ground. Pictures of The Skins were all over the walls, but there was one of Joe by himself that dwarfed them all. It was a poster, in fact, the size of a door, in color, of Joe at the beach. He'd grown all his hair back by then and had just come from the gym. Bennny caught me staring at the poster.

"He's a beauty, isn't he?"

"Yeah, he really is." (Little did he know, I thought. But then, maybe after all these years, he knew Joe as well as I did. I couldn't figure all that Joe was into, or all who may have been into Joe. I decided it would be fun to find out, for the memoirs.)

"So what do you really want to know?" he asked, snuffing out one cigarette and lighting another.

"About Paul."

He sighed, blew smoke in the air. "You would have loved him. Sweet kid. Real sweet kid. But it all started with Johnny. Johnny was our drummer and he'd OD'd once before and they just saved his ass. Then he went through counseling and stuff but then one night he was out alone and -well, he had to go to jail, no amount of money would get him out of it. It was just for driving while under the influence but he would have had to do three weeks, just three weeks. He couldn't live with that! He was willing to die to avoid that! His death was a serious setback-not just in the sense of losing a friend and all that but it was all of a sudden - boom! We found a new drummer but it wasn't the same. It wasn't his fault. It was just that it was hard being a new person around us."

"And Paul."

"When Paulie died Joe's whole world collapsed. It was the truly final blow." He looked away, out the window. "His love for Paulie had entered his soul. Now he has it forever. It's the one certainty in life that can be never taken away from him. Paul loved him till the day he died. And Joe loved Paul but he could never express it, physically or any other way than just be his friend."

He finished his cigarette, looking me up and down, then hard in the eyes. "I'm glad you came up here today. I feel better about it now." He moved from behind his desk for the first time and stood in front of me. His smile was nice, but there was desperation there, too, like he wanted me but knew it was impossible.

He seemed so desperate in his desire that it reminded of me when I was little and a rat got caught in a sticky open roach trap. The racket dragged me from my sleep and into the kitchen. When I turned the light on his scream was so loud I held my hands over my ears. I realized that he may have been a rat but he was as afraid of dying as we humans are. And, as he pressed himself deeper and deeper into the gluey trap, I went outside and got a shovel and was able to end his misery. In my dreams, animals would never die.

Benny leaned against his desk and ran his hand down his thigh. "You know, you remind me of Paul back in the beginning, except you're prettier. When I saw you, I thought, maybe now Joe's doing what he should've done ten years ago with Paul."

"At least he's not dying any more."

"What?"

"When I met him, he had this thing about dying."

"Oh, I know. He's been preoccupied with that for years. When he was on all the little girls' lunch boxes and the poster was the best-selling one of the year and all that -"

"That poster?" I asked, pointing to the one on the wall.

"Yeah."

"I'd love one. Do you have another one?"

He laughed. "Hell no. I wish I did. They say collectors' are getting fifty bucks for one these days. Anyhow, he had this thing about rock stars dying young. You know, Morrison, Joplin, all the rest. I'd kid him, 'Rock 'n' roll will never die, but when those who play it do, it's good for business,' and he'd laugh like hell but I know he thought I was just waiting for him to die. And then Johnny went and then Paulie. It was a nightmare for him. It was as if the public was waiting to see which one would go next. Everybody had Joe marked and, you know, there's a certain charisma about a guy that everybody thinks is about to drop dead. It's like when Daffy Duck blows up onstage and then you see him as an angel in heaven saying, 'Yeah, folks, it's a great show, but you can only do it once.'"

"Well, I'm happy he's not dying any more."

"You must be something," he said, his hand coming to rest on his crotch.

"No, it's not me," I said, preparing to leave. "It's Joe that's somethin'. Somethin' else."

"You don't know the half of it, kid. But I have a hunch you'll find out."

*

"I have an appointment to see Mrs. Skinner," I said.

"I'll see if she's free," the funny little receptionist said, giving me the once-over. Just as she began to open the left door of the big double doors, a tall, slender woman came out.

"You have a visitor," the receptionist said.

"Oh," Luisa said, her eyes drinking me in. "You must be little William."

Nodding, I gulped.

"Right this way," she said, pushing the double doors open.

"Take my calls. I may be a while," she said to the receptionist, closing the doors behind her.

"...What's going on?" she asked after we were seated, me on the couch, she across from me in a big chair.

"I'm working on a story about Joe. Well, it's by Joe actually. I'm just taking notes."

"You are?" She was suprised I had no notebook.

"Yeah. I have a good memory."

I couldn't imagine Joe being married to this lady. She was like the woman in a movie I saw once, "The Fountainhead." Patricia Neal played her. She drove Gary Cooper crazy. I could see that's what this woman must have done to Joe. Joe said she was into women now. I bet that she fucked her women with the biggest dildo she could find. She told me about how she was working for CBS Records when they met at a charity thing and how she pursued him trying to get him to sign with her company but instead, she got Joe to marry her. It only lasted a few months. "The divorce took longer to get than the marriage lasted, thanks to Benny. Have you met Benny?"

I nodded.

"I'll bet old Benny liked you."

I nodded again.

"Well, you are a nice little kid. I didn't expect that."

"Thanks."

She lit a cigarette, then clear out of the blue she said, "Joe's nuts about you."

"You think so?"

"Oh, yes," she said, taking a long drag. "When he called me and told me he wanted me to see you, I knew. I knew there was something good happening with him. It was in his voice. He's happy. I knew when he loved me and when he stopped. First he was happy, then he was unhappy. It didn't happen overnight but it didn't take long. Joe needs simplicity in his life. Everything's so hectic around him, he needs to come home to something simple." She sighed. "Yeah, I guess I know Joe better than anybody and I always knew, eventually, it would be a boy. 'Girls are too complicated,' he'd say. Yeah, a boy. A boy with a nice, squeezable ass. No, I'm never wrong about these things." She took another drag of her cigarette then asked me, "What more do you want to know?"

"I was just told I should meet you. That you might be able to give me a few quotes about Joe that would help the book."

"A few quotes? Look, kid, I could write a whole book all by myself, and I might some day. But what is it that he wants me to say? What couldn't he ask me himself?"

"It's about Paul. He said he never knew how you felt and he was afraid to ask you."

"I know he'd never do anything to hurt Paul. Whatever happened, it was an accident. Joe had nothing to do with it. Paul loved him. Joe had to live with that. Every day he had to live with that. And he lived with it very well. Nobody wanted Paul in the band but Joe stuck up for him. He wouldn't listen to the other guys. Paul was so mixed up. When Johnny died, Paul went bananas, saying he'd go the same way, and sure enough he did. But Joe had nothing to do with it. With either of them. Joe was at a party with me the night it happened. I told all that to the police, at the inquest, to the newspapers. What more could I do?"

I shrugged. "You couldn't have done any more."

"No. And Joe's never forgotten that, either. I have my business because of Joe. He set me up, paid for my condo." She chuckled. "Joe's a better ex-husband than he was a husband."

I smiled.

"You're lucky. You won't have to go through a marriage and then a divorce. You can just leave when the bed grows cold."

I frowned.

"Oh, it will, you know. He's restless. He bores easily. He must have had more roadies than any performer in history. And they can eat you alive. He never thought about it, it was just part of it. Now he's regretting it when some of them come out of the woodwork like that woman now, what's her name?"

"Brenda. Brenda Bartholomew."

"Yeah. What a joke. She's probably got Joe confused with somebody else. Maybe Jeffrey. Now he's the one you oughta talk to."

"Oh?"

"He's the one that hated Paul. Wanted him gone. I think they were all stuck on Joe, if you want to know the truth. Joe had this macho thing and they all wanted to challenge it but none of 'em would dare and then when Paul went to Germany and came out, well, that was it! They thought it would look bad, that it would make all of them look like they were sissies so that's why they wanted him to leave. When Joe wouldn't hear of it, well, then they started to wonder what was really going on between the two of them. It was all so incestuous! If they hadn't been so homophobic and all slept together, none of it would have happened. That's my opinion." She laughed. "And now Joe's a star again, all by himself, and he's got a cute little boy besides! Jeffrey would die!"

"Where is Jeffrey?"

"New York. He owns his own theater there, putting on little musicals, strictly off off Broadway, but it keeps him off the streets and out of the clubs. Benny invested his royalties for him and he can afford to do anything he wants. You know, they were making twenty million a year in old days." She looked me up and down again. "And from what I hear, Jeffrey's into lots of weird stuff himself now. But I doubt he could top what Joe has. That was the trouble, he never could top what Joe had."

*

"Squeezable," she said. "Squeezable ass." I kept repeating it in the limo as Harold was taking me back to the house. Joe had never asked me to roll over and I wondered why.

As we slowed in a traffic jam, I ran the tapes back in my mind. I saw how it happened. She was a woman who wouldn't take no for an answer. She strangled Joe. He wanted what he had been taught to want, a wife, but then he didn't. Damned if I could figure what he wanted, but I was determined just to give him what I knew he liked as often as he wanted it.

"Harold, you know where Joe's billboard is?"

"Yes, sir."

"Let's drive by it, and then let's go back down Santa Monica."

"Yes, sir."

I chuckled. Good old Harold.

Benny was right. They used the picture from the album cover. How jock can you get? Benny had told me, "They're gonna spend a million on promotion and a million on the video." "He's worth it," I said.

We took the long way home and went down Santa Monica. I didn't recognize a soul on the street. It was as if the cast had changed completely. Same old show, though. The little waves we got from guys trying to flag us down as we cruised by were so outrageous I laughed like hell but as we turned onto Mulholland and began our climb into the hills, I got real quiet, thinking about Kenny, wondering what had happened to him, thinking about how far away all of that seemed to me now in just a few days. Harold asked me what was wrong.

"Oh, nothing really. I'm just happy."

"You don't look happy." He was sneaking looks at me in the rearview mirror. I'd been noticing him noticing me more and more. I had begun to think he knew the score but shit with him I didn't need.

"Oh, I'll be happy when Joe gets home."

"He's quite something, isn't he?"

"Yeah, incredible."

"You're a lucky boy."

"Yeah, that's why I'm so happy."

He looked in the mirror again, longer this time. "Yes, now you look happy. Just talking about him makes you happy, doesn't it?"

"Well, he's my uncle, you know, and I'm glad to be here and I'm glad he's making a movie." I figured I'd better stick to the story. I wasn't sure about Harold. When I got out of the car and closed the door, he slid down the window and asked, "Will you be needing me tomorrow?"

"You'll have to ask Joe," I replied, with a big shit-eatin' grin on my face.

*

"...How was Luisa?" Joe asked me when he got home.

"Fine. But, you know, I was beginnin' to wonder that myself, while I was talking to her."

"Wonder what?"

"How she was."

He laughed. "A ball buster, that's what she was. Never stopped moving. I'd have to pin her down."

I slipped between his thighs. "You'll never have to pin me down."

"No, it's the other way around, isn't it?"

"You like it that way, with me pinning you down."

"Yeah, that's the way I like it." He locked his thighs around me and kissed me.

"...When did it start, your liking it that way?" I asked after I'd fucked him.

"In Mexico, after Paul died. I went on a long vacation. I'd read about Spanish men and I wanted to find out."

"What about 'em?"

"They're macho, they fuck and that's all they do. There's no kissing, caressing, they're just there to get their rocks off. That's what I wanted. I don't know why, just to find out what it was like. When I was in high school, it had been a fantasy of mine. A couple of guys I knew on the football team I would have taken to bed, believe me. But I didn't understand why. It was against everything I'd ever been taught. And then when I found out Paul was really into it I couldn't believe it."

"Paul wanted you, didn't he?"

"I suppose." He hugged me tighter. "I could have, hundreds of times, but it just wasn't right. We were always with other people, never alone. I guess I made sure that was the way it was, once I knew for sure that's what he was into." He sipped his Jack Daniels and thought a while. Then he went on: "I'm going to tell your tape recorder things I wouldn't tell you."

"Okay." I wanted to tell him I really wanted to know, that knowing would turn me on like crazy but I didn't. I just listened.

"Well, I've always been into watching. I sometimes think I'd rather watch than anything else."

"So I've noticed, in the mirrors."

"Yeah, I've gotta have a mirror. Now that you're here maybe I'll get one for the ceiling, too. Anyhow, sometimes it would be the three of us, Jeffrey, Paul and me, and these girls, sometimes four or five of them, all in the room, running from one of us to the other. We were so high it was hard to tell which one was which but it didn't matter."

"You were really into the drugs then, eh?"

"Yeah. But now, well, I don't know. I've been round and round with the drug thing. People are always wanting me to take a stand on drugs. I can't. To me, it's so relative, so personal. A person's relationship to drugs is like their relationship to sex. I mean, who's so all high and mighty that they can say, 'This guy's cool, this guy's not?'"

"George Bush."

"Yeah, sure. And Jesse Helms. But for me, all kinds of drugs have been both useful and a hindrance to me. But cocaine and heroin, those are the dead-enders. If someone could figure out how to do them without getting strung out, or without having them take over, then fine, but they haven't. I don't want to be a slave to any drug. I'm hopeful they'll come up with some good drugs, drugs that'll make you feel good and make you smarter."

"Smart drugs?"

"Yeah, if somebody said a drug would make me smarter, I'd say, 'No shit? Give me that.'"

"No shit."

"But now I got sex, that's the best drug of all," he said, climbing over me. He got into position and backed down on my prick. "Oh, God, you make me feel so fuckin' good."

I started moving my hips, sending my cock into him as far as it would go. "Best drug in the world, right?"

"...So," I said, coming out of the bathroom after washing up. He was still in bed, catching his breath. "You were on drugs with all these girls in the room and you - "

"Yeah, and I noticed that what Paul liked best was watching me ball some chick. He gave me the creeps at first having him watching but I decided it was better than other things that I didn't want to think about at the time. We were all so afraid of each other, afraid of coming out to each other, of what we really wanted. We believed our own publicity, I guess. And Benny saw to it that there were always plenty of girls. The boys he kept for himself. That was really hysterical. The boys would come and Benny would promise to introduce them and they'd spend the night with him and we'd be gone before they woke up. It was cruel but it was about the only way Benny could score."

He got up and poured himself another one, a short one, and I got a beer. "Oh," he chuckled, "I need to soak my ass." And we moved to the hot tub.

"...Yeah, I wanted to understand Paulie's pain. To feel his pain. Believe me, I found pain in Mexico. I enjoyed it there. I could walk around freely, nobody knew who I was. I didn't have to wear shades. I could let my hair grow really long. In Mexico City I met a guy who worked in a bank. He was what they call a loca, that's Spanish for queer, and he told me that he only wanted a man with a big cock who was masculine because he loved to have it inside of him. But he was upset because all they did was get off and leave. 'What am I supposed to do?' he asked. All he wanted was a fuck and I didn't want that. So he introduced me to one of his boyfriends, a man who was engaged to be married. He said he was going to love being married but he didn't know if he could ever give up boys because there was something different about having sex with them. 'But I know I'm not one of those locas because I only like to coger,' which is their word for fuck. 'I tried it once,' he told me, 'to take it, but it hurt too much. And, besides, I no woman!'

"He told me that in the town where he came from all the men have sex with boys at one time or another. But the boys always paid them, just a little something. It worked the opposite way in Mexico City, where the whores, the chichifos, always get paid for letting men fuck them. He said where he came from, men would hunt the boys up so they could get money to buy booze. They have a saying, 'Any hole is good, even if it's a man's.'"

"And so you had your first with this man?"

"Yes. Cortez. He was very gentle with me and we spent many nights together. He introduced me to many other men, but always with him in the room. I sometimes took on two or three in a night, altogether, one after the other, but after a while he said we were becoming enculado, which is to be joined by the anus, and he broke it off. But I came back to the States a happier man. And now look at me."

He rose from the steamy water and damned if his cock wasn't rigid again, pointing heavenward at the damndest angle I'd ever seen. It was a strange looking cock, very white, very thick but with a small head. It wasn't as long as mine, but it was as thick and as I slipped it into my mouth, I wondered what it would be like to take it up my ass. Suddenly, I was jealous of all the girls. For the first time, I was willing to admit I desired a guy that way. And I wanted it to be Joe. To become *enculado* with Joe.

From the LP "I Remember You"/Sung by Joe Skinner/Side 2, Cut 3,
"Fairy Tales:" "...I can remember stories, those things my mother said /
She told me fairy tales, before I went to bed / She spoke of happy endings,
then tucked me in real tight / She turned my night light on, and kissed my
face good night / My mind would fill with visions of perfect paradise..."

It seemed time passed so quickly I hardly noticed there were only
two weeks to go on the filming of Disney's alien epic, the title of
which had been changed three times during the shooting of it. Joe
shook his head, "They told me I could sing the title song, but they
don't even have a title let alone a song!" I thought about all the
movies I'd seen and wondered what had gone on behind the
scenes; I guess it's a wonder they got made at all.

There was some talk of going on a tour to promote the new LP.
I didn't want to think about the tour. I didn't want to ask about it,
for fear Joe would tell me I couldn't go. Then, out of the blue, he
says, "We're going to New York tomorrow."

As usual, I didn't know what to say so I didn't say anything.

"I've agreed to make an appearance at the New York Film
Festival. They're showing my first movie, can you believe it?"

I hadn't even seen his first movie, which ended up being released
as "Private People." He didn't even own a copy of it he hated it so
much and we're going to New York to celebrate it? "No, I can't
believe it," I replied.

"Oh, you'll love New York. Benny said he'd go with us. My folks
are in Europe so I'm going to have the company plane come out and
get us and fly us to New York."

It was the first time he'd mentioned his parents. I had to know
more: "The company plane?"

"Paper. Daddy's big in paper, didn't I tell you?"

"In Alabama?"

"Tuscaloosa. The only place to be big in paper. The only place.
But you gotta have your own plane, so you can leave."

It had begun to dawn on me that he'd always had everything he
wanted and, although it had been hard work being a singer and

being on the road, he put up with it because he loved the spotlight. He said: "After the first album hit and the teen magazines started on us, it was wild. Just walking out on stage they screamed for us. I could hear them screaming my name, not paying attention to what I was singing, nothing but me. I wanted them to like me but I realized they loved me. And it was great. They didn't even know me and they loved me. If they had known me, they would have hated me, but as long as I was my image, they loved me."

He never really suffered to become a star the way others did, and because things came easily for him, he could discard them easily. With each new day I wondered how long it would go on, this dream I was in, how long before he'd trade me in on a new model. But now he was actually saying I was going to New York with him. He'd never taken me out, other than to drive out Sunset to the Pacific Coast Highway and then up to Malibu on a Sunday to watch the sun setting over the sea. And with his eyes hidden behind his shades and baggy clothes hiding his brawn, we were just like any other couple. But now he was taking me to New York. In his parents' plane. It wasn't happening, yet it was.

*

It was a small white jet with a big red S on the tail of it. The two pilots paid me no mind at all and treated Joe like he was a member of the family, which I guess he was.

As we were taking off, it began to rain but soon we were flying above the rainclouds. Sunshine streamed into the cabin. A few raindrops clung on the windows and they sparkled when the sunlight caught them.

Joe gave me a beer and when I gulped it, he and Benny laughed. "You're not nervous, are you, kid?" Benny asked, patting my knee.

"Who me?" And I laughed harder than either of them.

Still, I was terrified. Only a few months before, I had never even been to the bus terminal. So many places I'd never been. When I told Pa I was going to take a bus to Hollywood he said, "You can't be serious. Now, no more nonsense. You're always talkin' nonsense." I chuckled to think what kind of nonsense he'd think this was, flying across the Grand Canyon in the Skinner Industries' jet, with the guy I thought to be handsomest man in the world sitting across from me, pouring me another beer.

Suddenly, I felt very comfortable. Benny and I sat facing Joe. There was a table between us where we put our drinks and Joe was reading the latest issue of *The New Yorker* while Benny and I talked.

After Joe told the pilot to "buzz the Canyon," Joe began reading us an article about a new club that had opened in New York and Benny broke in: "...Celebrities go to places like that now. We could never do that in the old days. But still, there's such a stigma attached to being gay and it's worse today, with AIDS. I hate that. I can live with being a Jew but being gay is something I could never deal with. It doesn't mean a thing, it's just an aspect of my life, that's all. I hate ghettos, making tiny islands in the middle of humanity. Jews do that, gays do that. And like the Jews, most of the gays today have lost touch, they don't try to communicate, to tell people that they are not a threat to society. They're as uptight about straights as straights are about them. Us, we're in-between, aren't we Joe?"

Joe chuckled. "If you say so."

"Yeah, in-between. Hey, what's that word they used to describe you guys in the beginning?"

"Androgynous."

"Yeah, that's what they always called the boys, androgynous."

"We could go either way," Joe said, closing his magazine, shifting slightly in his seat and then winking at me.

"But it was Paulie who went every which way. Yeah, he and Johnny, they were always into excess. If you said jump two feet, they'd jump ten."

"Paulie taught me the big rule, though," Joe said, taking another magazine up from the seat next to him.

"Yeah?"

Joe looked up, his eyes sparkling. "Yeah, that there are no rules. Every rule can be broken." And he winked at me again.

4

Joe had the pilot "buzz the City" and as we came down through the mist it was like a Polaroid picture, printing before my eyes. The City was exposing itself to me, glittering and showy and everything I'd ever imagined it would be from seeing it for years on TV. Joe identified all the biggest buildings and the Park. "Our hotel's right there, on the edge of it," he said, pointing to the Plaza.

"We'll have to stop staying there, Joe. Trump's going to turn it into condos."

"So buy one of 'em."

"I'll make a note of it."

Benny was always making a note of everything Joe said, although he never wrote anything down.

"You'll feel at home in Manhattan. Most of the people have dyslexia," Joe said. "But they aren't like you. They never get any help. You've risen above 'em. They're all still stuck on their rock."

"On the brink of nervous breakdown," Benny chimed in. "Still, it's a fun place to visit."

Joe smiled. "Like Johnny used to say, in New York you've gotta just 'let it ride.'"

I knew Joe'd be doing a lot of riding in New York, riding my prick for all it was worth. I wondered if they had any mirrors at the Plaza, then I decided they must have or Joe wouldn't stay there.

*

In the glare of the klieg lights, I saw a different Joe Skinner. He was transformed into the star I saw in the music videos from the late '70s and early '80s he kept at the house, the star I imagined on stage. He waved to the crowd, smiling, loving every minute of it. I walked silently behind Benny. Joe had a "date" for the night, a starlet named Dorianne Dempsey, who accompanied him onstage while he answered questions from the audience.

At one point he said: "I'll never forget this film because Alec Guinness has a cameo bit as a homeless man in London right at the beginning...He was great, wonderful to work with, so many jokes. And he gave me a lot of confidence because he told me he's always very nervous, very unsure of himself. He told me it never goes away, that insecurity."

"Lack of confidence doesn't seem to have been a problem with you," someone said.

"Oh, yes, from the beginning. Appearing on stage, in front of a bunch of screaming girls, is terrible. But being in a movie, with real actors, people who have been doing it for years, is even spookier. Every time I see this movie I wonder why I did this or that in it. Luckily, I didn't have many lines to learn. You know, the truly perfect movie has no dialogue. That's what they were trying for...Yeah, this is an action picture like no other. All in bed or in the shower or on the balcony!"

I thought, like me and Joe at the house on the cliff, and I closed my eyes, remembering, wishing I was back there. Now, seeing him make love to some girl on the big screen, even if it was make-believe, was not my idea of fun.

Joe and the girl sat together at the beginning of the movie, then left. I started to follow them but Benny said we had to stay. "It's cool," he said. I believed everything Benny said because he was so final about it. You never argued with Benny. If Benny had forced it, I figured, I might have been history.

"It was pretty bad, kid, " Benny said on our way out. "I don't remember it being that bad, Alec Guinness or no Alec Guinness. Joe really can't act worth shit, you know?"

"He was beautiful, though," I said. "Especially when he was naked."

Benny smiled. "Yes, he was."

"I meant, Mr. Kaplan, that Joe is beautiful." (I always called him Mr. Kaplan. He loved it, I could tell. "Kid's got respect," he told Joe once.)

"Yes," he said, grinning, "he certainly is, kid. He certainly is."

We found Joe and the girl at the little bar in the lobby, laughing and joking like a couple of lovebirds. I would have been insane with jealousy but I knew who Joe was going to take back to the suite at the Plaza, who he would be sleeping with that night and it wouldn't be her.

I stood next to a man in a tuxedo who was gabbing on a cellular phone while Joe posed for photographs with the starlet and with some of the girls who came to the showing. I asked one of them what she saw in Joe and she just groaned, unable to put it into words. Another said, "Oh, he's got such a cute butt."

That really made my day. If she had known what I was doing to that cute little butt every night she would've had a heart attack. But, of course, that was the point of the whole deal. We were like characters on the screen only we were off the screen...but not very far.

Joe politely signed autographs and then said to Benny, "Give me air." Benny nodded and we began our move toward the door. Benny had many years of experience getting Joe in and out of a crowd and we just kept moving, steadily toward the door, slicing through the crowd, and in moments we were back in the limo.

Benny and I sat in the jump seats and Joe and the girl sat across from us. They were still laughing and joking. I decided Joe was a better actor than anybody gave him credit for. Benny fixed everybody a cocktail and by the time we got to what Joe called "Cafe Lux," actually Cafe Luxembourg on 70th Street, the girl was falling all over Joe. But he told the driver to take her back to "wherever she came from" and then call for us in an hour or so. "Give me air," Joe sighed as we were going into the restaurant.

While one problem was disposed of, another awaited us at the Lux. I wasn't told that Joe had invited his old partner Jeffrey for a reunion. After I was introduced and we were seated in a deep red booth in the back of the room, Benny and Jeffrey were head-to-head talking and I whispered to Joe that I thought it would be better if I left. He just shook his head and, under the table, took my hand and held it. I guided it to my crotch and he left it there for a few moments and I grew stiff under his magic touch. Everything was going to be fine, he was saying. From the looks I was getting from Jeffrey, I wasn't so sure. Finally, Jeffrey acknowledged my presence by asking, "So, how long have you been in Hollywood?"

"Just a couple of months."

"Not long enough to have acquired any bad habits, eh?"

"Well, maybe a couple." I smiled, looking at Joe. I thought it best to smile. Joe quickly changed the subject, talking about the festival.

Jeffrey's date was an Italian actress named Carmen, a tall woman in her 30's with brown hair streaked blond. She wore a man's dinner jacket. I never caught the last name but if I ever see her in a movie I'll recognize her and be able to say I had dinner with her.

When we first arrived, she was in the rest room so we all had a chance to get acquainted before she re-appeared. Everybody in the place watched her as she moved through the room to where we were sitting and when she sat down, Jeffrey said, "Joe's always wanted to meet you."

Joe laughed. Not five minutes earlier he'd said he'd never heard of her.

"Oh?" she asked, squeezing into the booth next to Jeffrey.

"Yeah, he read you like men with power," Jeffrey said.

"Oh, no, that's not true at all. I don't like powerful people. Oh, I've liked some, but, generally, no. But I do have to admit I like to wield my own power over others."

"Does she ever -" Jeffrey laughed.

"Yes, I'm a monstrous individualist. I can't work up interest in others and I can't be influenced by the men I'm with. I am curious about their life but then I grow bored."

"Does she ever," Jeffrey kidded. "She's bored with me already and she's only been in town three days."

"I have to come to New York once a year. I love it. You meet such interesting people here. Jeffrey knows such interesting people."

"Thanks. I think," Jeffrey laughed.

"No, I love artists," she said, smiling at Jeffrey. "Their work is immortal."

"Are you staying at Jeffrey's?" Joe asked.

"Oh no, heavens no. At the Palace. I love hotels. If I had enough money, I'd live in hotels all the time. And I always sleep alone."

"Really?" Jeffrey asked.

"Oh, you know what I mean. I hate to sleep with someone. In the morning, if I've slept with someone, I feel unclean."

"Nothing worse," Joe muttered.

"What's your favorite hotel?" I asked. She seemed shocked I was even entering into the conversation but I was fascinated.

"Oh, I suppose the Mamounia in Marrakesh."

I nodded as if I knew all about it. I wasn't even sure I knew where Marrakesh was. "Yes, I've heard it's nice," I said.

Joe chuckled. "When in Rome - "

"Oh, the Cavalieri Hilton on Monte Mario," she gushed. "I love the pool."

While they chatted away, I watched Jeffrey in the mirrors all around. He caught my eye several times and smiled. I just sat there as if I belonged, nibbling on the crunchy sourdough rolls and listening, committing what they said to the tapes in my mind, nodding at times as if I really understood. And maybe I understood more than they thought I did.

I remembered what Joe had said about Jeffrey, and especially what Luisa had said, that he was weird. And then that Jeffrey had invited Luisa and Joe to a place in the mountains for a weekend and how they got high and at some point they switched partners and when Joe saw Jeffrey fucking his wife he freaked. He got up and said, "That's it, we're leaving." Joe put it this way: "Nobody fucks Luisa but me. Her doing it with another girl I could live with, but not another guy, especially my best friend." He didn't speak to

Jeffrey for a couple of weeks and then he didn't blame Jeffrey, he blamed Luisa.

Finally, Carmen said she was hungry and Jeffrey called the waiter. She ordered salmon and more champagne and we all had the same. After the waiter left, she said, out-of-the-blue, "You can live without sex, you just can. You absolutely can sustain life without sex."

"Yeah, you can, but who would want to?" Jeffrey laughed.

"Oh, sexual tension's everywhere. I feel it?"

"Yeah," Joe snickered. I beamed.

"Oh, and I support it. But I don't partake of it all the time."

"Only when in New York - " Jeffrey chuckled.

"Well, you know, when you go out maybe seven times out of ten a situation occurs because somebody was giving off this wonderful energy that somebody else was picking up on. And you just seize the moment."

"Yeah, that's what I do all the time, seize the moment," Joe chuckled, squeezing my crotch.

I drank some more champagne. Things were finally getting interesting.

"You've all read the papers and know what I've done and what I haven't done. It's so bizarre! Why the fuck would anybody care? And when they completely fabricate something it really blows your mind."

"Yes," Joe said. "I've seen years of my life summed up in five sentences. It sounds like it all took place over this wild weekend."

"Was all a blur to me," Jeffrey laughed.

Carmen chuckled. "I've read flat-out lies so hideous but I stopped reading it because I wasn't going to let them get to me. Give me a fucking break."

"You've had some great romances, though, Carmen. Marcello and even David Bowie!"

"Oh, God! I spend twenty hours a day on a set with this person for three months out of my life and I know him, right? I sure as hell know him better than somebody I tried to make time to see maybe three times in those three months.

"I think a complete relationship can last a week if you walk away with something that you don't forget or something that moved you or something that altered you. "

"It makes for interesting conversation at lunch in Hollywood, though. Like, 'Well, I just saw Joe Skinner and he was drunk again.' 'And what did he do this time?' They get seven minutes of glory and I look like shit."

Carmen nodded. "It's all part of this mass insanity. It's a mass sickness, this interest people have in us, their jealousy, their envy."

"It's like a kind of disease," Joe said. "I don't have an entirely objective view of what that is, but I do have pretty good idea of what people think of me now - that I was this teen idol and then I became a drunk and now I'm a two-bit actor making cameo appearances in other people's movies." He laughed. "Once I was trying to make a call on a house phone in a hotel and this guy comes up to me and asks, 'Hey, man, are you as big a drunk as they say?' And I said, 'Yeah.' It takes longer if you try to defend yourself."

"They're cowards," Jeffrey said. "They don't look at the truth."

"It's as if they realized that the wolves needed some food so they said, 'Hey, here's this kid, name's Joe Skinner. Have a feast.'"

I looked at him and chuckled to myself, realizing how few people really knew what a fucking feast he was.

"Well, with this new album and this new movie, you'll have the last laugh, Joe."

"Yeah. You know, I dearly love rock music when it's good, but it really wasn't me. I'm pop rock, for chrissakes, really an old-fashioned, sentimental piece of shit. Sure, you can say what the hell is this shit in the new album, but I think these songs are talking about the kind of love everybody wants."

"I love it," I chimed in.

Joe smiled. "Yeah, it's like Dylan has written songs that touch into places people have never sung about before and I admire that. But I can't write 'em, I can only sing 'em."

"And dance. You sure could dance. Yeah, we had it all then," Benny said, "Jeffrey on keyboard, best in the business. Johnny on drums. And Paulie on guitar, unreal. And Joe, he was on stage only half the time, singing and dancing, carrying on."

"Well, I can't just stand on stage. I feel like an idiot most of the time. It was like getting up in front of the senior class when I was elected president and making my little speech. I need these songs, these powerful kind of songs, as an armor I can hide behind."

"Yeah, when we went out onstage and started the music, it was if we were transformed, from these ordinary guys into something like forces of a larger consciousness. And the audience wants that,

75

they don't want reality, they want fantasy, and we gave 'em that. They never knew what to expect next."

"And we all got along."

"Yeah, because, the thing was, we treated each other like equals."

"Sure we did," Jeffrey laughed. "The thing was, I learned to always get out of the van first because once Joe got out, all hell broke loose."

"Really? I thought all the commotion was for Paulie."

"Paulie, shit."

"I seem to have problems wherever I go," Joe said. "But now I kinda miss it, I really do, but it's scary being on your own. But I just couldn't go on after Paulie died. I just couldn't. All I needed was people yelling, 'Sit down, man, you're a fuckin' disgrace.' So now I'm taking more heat for doing something ambitious than other people get for just cashing it in. The truth is I did this because I wanted to, not to get anybody's approval."

"And it's great, it really is. Shit, man, I wish I'd been on keyboard for you."

"You weren't available, remember?"

"Yeah, yeah."

"But that's why I wanted to come to New York, to see if I could convince you to do this little tour with me, just twelve cities in a month. No big deal. Just play the piano. As if we were in a saloon."

"I'll think about it."

After dinner, Jeffrey invited us to a party. "You oughta expose the kid to some theatrical types," Jeffrey chuckled.

"Sure, why not," Joe said. And we were off in the limo.

It was a small apartment, beautifully furnished, and the host, a balding queeny type, Eddie, was thrilled Joe could make it. "You must sing for us," he gushed.

"Only if I get paid," Joe laughed, brushing past him. "Where's the bar?"

The host pointed into the dining room, introduced Benny to a guy bulging out of his Gold's Gym tank top, and then turned his attention to me. I thought I looked pretty good in my dark blue Ralph Lauren blazer and tight chinos but this guy really got off on it, saying how things had really changed since he went to college. "They really wear clothes like that at Ohio State?"

"Sure," I said. "Every day."

He led me from room to room introducing me as Joe's nephew

from Ohio State.

"He's too little to be a football player," one guy said.

"Maybe, but boy, does he know how to ball!" Eddie kidded.

Finally, Jeffrey left Carmen with some "artists" and rescued me. We sat on the little terrace looking out at the skyline, drinking champagne cocktails. I kept checking on Joe in the living room but eventually he disappeared. "What's wrong?" Jeffrey asked.

"Joe. He's had too much to drink again."

"Hey, you can't keep him on the wagon for long."

"So I've found out."

"Just like you can take the boy out of the country but you can't take the country out of the boy."

"Is it so obvious?"

"Yes, but you're not obvious. That's what appealed to Joe, I know. Shit, you look straighter than he does. You're so fresh, so honest, so trusting, you really look out of place here. It's almost as if you'd be out of place anywhere but the farm you came from."

"Is that bad?"

"No. I think when you've been to college and done everything Joe and I've done, well, you get old and tired and maybe even sick and things stop being new and exciting. To see you enjoying everything, to be so crazy about Joe, well, it's nice."

"Thanks." It was a surprise, his being nice. I suddenly liked him, liked him a lot. He wasn't as handsome as Joe but he had a certain quality about him, decidedly macho yet something I could work on. If Joe hadn't been there, I don't know what I would have done. But as it was, I got up and went to find my man. He was where I knew he would be, at the bar, pouring another Jack Daniels.

"I'm really tired -" I said.

"I'll bet," he said, "After Jeffrey now are you?" And when he turned to face me I saw the coldness was back in his eyes and I wanted to run again. I did just that, out the door without saying goodbye, looking for Benny, without stopping for anything. I took the stairs rather than wait for an elevator and instead of the limo I took a cab. When I got back to the Plaza they didn't want to give me a key to the room but I caused such a commotion they decided I must be with the Skinner party.

Less than an hour later, Joe threw open the door to the bedroom. I hadn't been sleeping, just lying there in bed wondering what would happen when he finally showed. He swayed back and forth as he came to the bed. He yanked the sheet away and saw that I was nude.

"You liked Jeffrey, didn't ya?"

"Jeffrey?"

"I saw you, smiling at him, turning it on for him. What can he do that I can't?"

"Hey, Joe, this is crazy! We were just talkin'."

"What can he do?" he insisted.

"Nothin'. He can't do anythin'."

"No, you're wrong. You're fucking wrong! He fucks! That's what he does best. He fucks! He fucks people over, he fucks around with the music, he fucks everything in sight. The girls love him because he's the best goddam fucker there ever was!"

I felt like saying, "If you say so," but I didn't. I just rolled over, ignoring him.

"Yeah, turn your pretty ass to me why don't ya? That's what you want, isn't it? You're just a little fairy, just a goddam little fairy, like all the rest. All ya want is to get fucked. You just live to get fucked."

I wanted to say, no, Joe, you're the one that lives to get fucked, but I didn't. I kept ignoring him. I heard him undressing. I hoped he'd pass out before he got naked but he didn't. He climbed on the bed and grabbed my ass, one cheek in each hand and spit between them. I tried to roll over. "No, Joe, not like this."

"The only way for you, fairy. The only way."

At first I squirmed, attempting to get away, but I knew he could easily   overpower me. He wanted it this way, I decided. And whatever he thought of me in the morning I would just have to deal with. It was as if we had created new characters just for the night. If I could live with that, it was okay. The room had a big, gilded mirror that Joe had taken off the wall earlier and propped up against some chairs so that he could watch me fuck him. Now with the dim light coming from the living room. I watched our reflections as he slapped my ass and fingered me. It was turning me on.

"Yeah, Jeffrey knows a good piece of ass when he sees it. But this one's mine. Shit, I've fuckin' paid for it a thousand times."

It always got down to that. He'd paid for it. That's all I was. A whore. I wanted to cry, "Yes, yes, only for you," but I didn't. I didn't say anything because I didn't know what to say. My father had taught me that.

I lifted myself up to meet Joe's fingers but he slammed me down.

He kept spitting, then took a bottle of champagne, left over from the afternoon, and poured it all over my ass, then began licking it off. He split my cheeks and poured it into me, followed by his fingers. He was rough and I cried out in pain. I kept squirming and the more I did, the more force he applied. He had shoved me up on the bed and pinned me against the headboard. Soon he was lying on top of me, sliding over me. His cock was semi-hard; he would get the head of it in my ass and but when he tried to stick more of it in, it slid out. I cringed with the pain a couple of times and that turned him on, but not enough to get a full erection. The champagne was gone and he threw the bottle into a corner. He continued to lick my skin, my shoulders, my back, then my ass again. Finally, I came when his tongue went into my ass. I couldn't help it; the pressure on my cock between the mattress and my abdomen was overwhelming. It wasn't a very intense orgasm, just a relief, but he felt my shuddering. He reached under me and ran his fingers along my prick, feeling the wetness.

"Yeah," he snarled, "this is what you've wanted all along isn't it?"

I didn't say anything.

"Isn't it?" He yelled in my ear, shaking me again.

"Yes, yes!"

"Yeah, that's right, sissy," he moaned and it seemed to satisfy him because he rolled across my back a few more times and then slid off of me onto the bed, finally passing out.

I staggered out of the bed and went to close the door to the bedroom. As I was shutting it, I looked into the living room of the suite and saw Benny was sitting on the couch. He had seen it all. I just stood there in the open doorway and made no attempt to hide my nakedness.

He shook his head. "I don't know how anybody can be so mean to someone as beautiful as you are."

I stepped into the room and dropped down into the big overstuffed chair across from him. I didn't know what to say so I didn't say anything.

"I know how tough it is being with these guys," he went on. "It wore me out. But you're young, you can handle it."

"Not many more scenes like that I can't. I just don't understand."

"I never did either. There's this terrible war going on in their minds and they try to make you a part of it. They succeed most of the time and then it's you that has to pay, not them."

I really looked at him for the first time. He had done so much for them and continued to do it, yet he took whatever was dealt him, and I knew he was trapped. What else could he do? He was over 40, ugly, with a terrible toupee, and he was willing to live his life through his band. But I had a choice. I could leave.

He stood up and began walking towards his bedroom. "Get some sleep. We'll have some fun tomorrow. There's some things I haven't seen here in years and I want to take you along."

"Okay," I said, closing my eyes.

*

When the cute room service boy rolled in the cart with a gold linen tablecloth on it, then very efficiently began laying the breakfast out, Benny took the newspaper off the cart. "Three places?" the kid asked, his eyes moving from me to Benny and back again.

I shrugged.

"Yes, three," Benny said, picking up the check from a silver tray and signing it. As he dropped the check back on the tray, he gave the boy a once over again, then looked at me and winked.

"Thank you," the boy said, "thank you very much," and then left with the little tray in his hand.

"Adorable ass," Benny said after he was gone.

Nodding, I drank my orange juice in one gulp then started in on the eggs and toast.

As he promised, Benny took me sightseeing while Joe slept it off. It was a gray day and the tops of the buildings were lost in a fog and he said, "The mist is the veil between this world and the other."

It started to rain and the people scurried along, the patterns of their umbrellas shifting like a weird video. The cars swished in the pothole puddles and the traffic lights blinked. As the rain started coming down sideways, Benny and I ducked into a coffee shop.

"This place is just too much, " I said. "It's everything I ever imagined and more."

"Are you?"

"Am I what?"

"More than anyone imagines?"

"Hardly."

"God, from what I saw last night, you're more than I'd ever

imagined. Talk about hung!"

He was looking at me in a new way, a greedy way. I avoided his eyes. "Let's not talk about last night."

When the rain stopped, we decided to take the ferry to the Statue of Liberty. Looking back at Manhattan I realized it really was an island and that all the people on it were trapped, forced to somehow get along with each other. There may have been bridges and airports so you could escape but, when you got right down to it, all those different races and sexual orientations had to get along. Looking at the island as it came and went in the mist I felt a rush of excitement that I didn't ever get in L.A.

When we returned, Joe was on the phone. Wrapped in his silk robe that matched my new one, he waved to us and went on talking. I took a beer from the refrigerator and sat down beside him on the couch. His eyes were bloodshot and his hair was damp from a shower but he still looked good enough to eat. I set my hand on his thigh. He picked it up and held it to his lips and nibbled my fingers as he listened.

"We'll see you tonight, after the concert. It'll be fun. Maybe I can even talk Diana into coming. Haha!"

He hung up the phone.

"Concert?"

"Diana Ross's opening at Radio City tonight. Jeffrey got us seats and then we're meeting him at his place after for a little buffet. He's become a gourmet cook. Can you believe it?"

He put his arm around me and drew me into him. As we were about to kiss, Benny said, "Excuse me. I'm going to take a nap."

"Benny doesn't like to watch," Joe said after he'd gone.

"Oh? News to me."

He did a doubletake, then said, "Yeah, Benny's very private. He goes off and does his own thing. Like tonight, he'll go to the concert but he'll beg off dinner."

He held me and looked out the window. "It's sad about Benny. He gets into dangerous scenes. I hope he buys something tonight that won't kill him." His eyes returned to mine and he reached down and took my cock in his hand. "God," he chuckled, "I bet this could kill Benny."

He was stroking it, admiring it, like he always did. It was as if the night before had never happened.

*

"...Don't ever let me get stale like that," Joe said to Benny after the concert. Benny was leading us backstage and there was a security guard behind us. No one recognized Joe, his face hidden behind his dark glasses.

Joe'd complained all during the performance about Miss Ross. "You should've seen her in the '70s," he said at intermission. "Now, that was a show. I saw her in Atlanta when I was a teenager. She was over-the-top, man, just unbelievable. This is shit. She doesn't even have a band, for chrissakes, just the synthesizers. She acts as if she's sleepwalking. Going, going, gone."

In the second half, with long black hair that flowed past his shoulders, a guy impersonating her tried to get onto the stage. The guards stopped him but Diana had him brought on. "Who are you?" she asked. "I'm Diana Ross," the guy said.

"No, you aren't me!" She wagged her finger at him. "Not with straight hair you're not!" Then she asked us which hair we liked better. I voted for the drag queen; Joe voted for Diana. Benny just shook his head. She won, of course, then had the guards get the guy off so she could sing her best number, "God Bless the Child." Benny leaned into me and whispered, "God bless you, child." I just grinned.

There was a crowd of people at the dressing room door and when she stepped out to shake hands, I saw she had changed into a sarong and looked small and somehow helpless amid the adoration. Joe talked with a couple of people he knew, people I didn't recognize, and Benny pointed out Tony Bennett and Billy Baldwin, whom I didn't know from Adam but probably should have. Soon Diana Ross was in front of us. Joe congratulated her, then introduced me as his nephew. She just touched my hand, not even shaking it really, and then gave Joe a little peck on the cheek. Quickly she moved on to some of the others standing behind us and we were on our way out the rear exit where the limo was waiting.

Joe was right about Benny; he had the driver drop him off at a bar called Rounds and we went on to the Village. Joe opened the car's bar and poured himself a Jack Daniels. I had a beer. "Here," he said, reaching into his coat pocket, "take this." He handed me a pill. "Jeffrey can always get the best pills."

"No. I don't do drugs, you know that."

"Just tonight. We're in New York, havin' a party."

I shook my head.

"Shit, you're worse than Benny! Now take one. You'll feel great. Trust me."

I wasn't going to swallow it, just make it look as if I did, but the tire of the limo hit a pothole in the road and the pill slipped down my throat anyway. Oh, shit, I thought, but then I was, after all, there to please him. If that's what he wanted. I put my head back and looked through the skylight of the limo. As the lights in the tall buildings twinkled as we sailed by them, I pinched Joe's knee just to reassure myself I wasn't dreaming.

Jeffrey lived on the top floor of a building he owned in the Village. On the first floor were his offices and the second and third were rehearsal halls. We went up in a freight elevator. The door opened right into a huge room, all white and chrome. There were about a dozen people there, boys and girls, all under 30. Joe found Jeffrey right away and left me with him to go directly to the bar. Jeffrey's handshake was dry and firm. He held my hand and sort of led me to the food buffet.

"Hey, you look like you're starvin'," he said. "I made all this just for you."

He didn't seem to want to stop touching me. When his hand left mine it was on my arm, then on my neck, then he squeezed me there. I turned and stared at him, as if to say, do you want something?

"You're a cute little bugger," he said, smiling.

"That's me, the bugger."

He blinked, as if he couldn't quite believe it. I knew about being bugged and being buggered. It dawned on me that he figured Joe was fucking me. Perhaps it was beyond his comprehension that Joe would take it up the ass. And he was beginning to bug me in another sense; if he showed any more interest in me and Joe saw us again, well, I didn't want to think about it. I looked around the big living room for my man. "Joe's at the bar in the kitchen," Jeffrey said. "If you want to know where Joe is, just listen for the ice cubes dropping in a glass."

He put his arm around my waist. "But we don't need him tonight, do we?"

I gulped.

"You know, you remind me of the boys in Paris. They're over 18 but they look like they're only fifteen. And they like girls as much as they like guys."

"I don't dislike girls," I muttered.

"Good."

The music blaring out of the speakers I recognized as early Skins. Jeffrey hollered to the boy at the stereo. "No, not that shit, not tonight. Put Joe's new CD on."

I shoved another one of Jeffrey's funny little gourmet meatballs in my mouth as he led me through the crowd beginning to form around the table. We ended up in a far corner of the room. "There's somebody I want you to meet," he said.

She was tiny, a little doll of a girl, with blond curls, wearing a "Bad Company" T-shirt ripped just so, enough to show a nipple, and black tights. Jeffrey introduced me as Joe Skinner's nephew and the girl, Tina, gushed, "Oh, you're even cuter than he is."

"It's in the genes -" Jeffrey snickered, slapping my ass. "All in the jeans."

"She's thinking about going to Hollywood," Jeffrey said. "Maybe you can discourage her." And he left us alone.

"It's so dark over here in this corner," I said, sitting next to her on a huge black cube.

"I don't like too much light," she said. "In fact, I don't like the sun. That's why I've turned down so many chances to go to California. Besides the radiation, it does a number on pesticides. Did you know that?"

"No."

She took a swig of something in a china cup and went on. "Besides I think things are nicer in the dark, don't you?"

"Yeah."

"I don't really plan it but I'm usually up all night. I get a lot more done that way, you know? Like, I don't need my sleep. None at all, really. And at night you pick up more signals."

"Signals?"

"Well maybe you people in California would call them vibes. I call them signals, like what's happening with us. Like when I saw you come in the door, I said to Jeffrey, that's it, that's my date for tonight. And he said, 'You mean Joe Skinner.' And I said, 'Hell, no, the cute little one with him.'" Her hand dropped to my thigh and she sighed, "It's all in the signals."

"Well, I got a date tonight, you know?"

"That's interesting, but let me go on." And she did, for what seemed like hours, talking shit, until I finally decided I'd better find Joe. But she followed along, saying she needed more tea.

"...Stimulants are important," Joe was telling some guy, "but I need to chill out sometimes, you know." He reached in his pocket and grabbed something, then opened his hand to the guy. "Red, yellow, blue. Name your flavor."

"I need a co-pilot tonight. And black. I like 'em black," the guy said.

"Oh," Joe said, reaching into his other pocket. "Here we are -"

"Yeah," the guy said, taking one of the black and white ones.

Wedging in between them, I said: "Tina needs more tea."

Joe gave her the once over with his bloodshot eyes and said, "She needs more 'n tea."

"Drugs?" the guy suggested.

"Just aspirin," Tina said, adjusting her ragged T-shirt so that both nipples showed. Her tits were small but beautifully formed. "I used to like PCP but, you know, sometimes you just come to the end of the scene."

"End of scene," Joe said, moving back to where the bottles were set up.

I went to him, touched his elbow and said, "Joe - "

Pouring another drink, he glared at me. "Hey, kid, Tina needs some tea."

I nodded, bit my lip, and went to look for the tea.

"...Let's find a darker place," Tina said, holding her china cup out in front of her and leading the way. She had me firmly by the hand. The red pill and the beer had gone to my head and my resistance was melting away. There were only two other rooms in the loft, one obviously Jeffrey's bedroom and the other a study with a wall of books and a black piano. We sat at the piano and she tried to play the song that was on the stereo, still Joe's CD, "I Remember You."

"That's such a pretty song," she sighed.

"His voice is so great; that's what makes it."

She stopped playing and finished her tea. "It puts me into a such a crazy mood. It's like I feel these terribly strong signals right now that we've got to do something. Can you feel it?" She put down her cup on the piano and pressed her body next to mine.

"No. Well, yeah, I feel strong signals like I'd better go find Joe."

"It's okay. Jeffrey told me it was cool. He said Joe'll play along.

That's what he wants, actually."

"What he wants?"

"Yeah, Jeffrey says he's got this thing about watching. He loves to watch. And it's the safest sex you can have, you know?" She kissed my chin and started rubbing my pecs. "And Jeffrey knows there's nothing I like better than an audience. That's why he invited me. I always get invited to his parties, one way or another."

"Life of the party, right?"

"Sweetie, sometimes I am the party."

As she was unbuttoning my shirt and pulling it from my pants, she asked, "What do you do for a living?"

"I hustle."

"I hustle, too, sweetie, but I'm really selling an essence. It's all essence."

"I'll have to remember that."

Suddenly, it seemed her essence was too close for comfort, but I was getting excited by the thought of it all the same. Her tit fell completely out of her ripped T-shirt and I took it in my hand. I'd seen plenty of movies; I knew how this was supposed to go, and I'd played around like this before when I was in high school with the girl who lived down the road. I'd messed around with her body, just to see what it was all about, and she really got off on it. I didn't fuck her. I didn't have to. She just went crazy without my sticking her at all.

But now I didn't feel as if I wanted to please Tina. It was as if from that point on it was as if I was pleasing Joe. That eventually he'd come in and do what she said, watch. And the thought of him watching me, for some reason, turned me on. I pulled her T-shirt over her head and threw it in a corner, then started kissing her tits, playing with her nipples, which were really hard after awhile. She climbed over me and slid her thighs around me and rubbed her crotch against mine. And there, on the piano bench in the dark, she rubbed against me and kissed me and ran her hands through my hair as if I was the sexiest thing in the world. Suddenly, the music stopped and I could hear people leaving. Then the music started again, the old Skins music again. I heard footsteps down the hall and then Jeffrey was in the room. He turned on a small lamp on his desk.

"I knew you two'd get along," he said, dropping down on the bench behind Tina.

"He's so hot," Tina gushed, pulling my shirt further apart and kissing my chest.

Jeffrey was rubbing her back and I looked at him and shrugged.

"Yeah," he said, "Joe was right about him. He's a hot little number."

As she worked her way down my chest to my navel, I leaned back on my elbows. She unzipped my pants and exposed my dick, now fully erect.

"God, sweetie, little he ain't."

Jeffrey looked around her, glanced down at my cock swaying in front of her face, and snickered, then lifted her up and started to pull her black tights down her butt. She bent over even further, took my cock in her hand and kissed the shaft. He tugged and tugged at her tights but finally just ripped them apart. She moaned and pulled my balls out of my pants.

I heard footsteps again. Just in time, I thought. I still had time to cover up and get the hell out of there. I pulled away and stood up. My cock was arching in her face and Jeffrey had his hands on her middle, pushing her toward me. Just then, Joe appeared next to me, taking me in his arms. I fell against his chest and turned my face toward him. He swayed back and forth with the music and just held me. Tina opened her mouth and started taking my cock between her lips. Jeffrey lifted her up again and got her on her knees on the piano bench, pulling what was left of the black tights down around her knees. Joe's hand moved to my balls and he played with them while she sucked me. I kissed his chest and tried to squirm away and turn toward him but he held me tight, forcing me deep into her throat. I looked over her body and saw Jeffrey undo his pants and slip out his hard rod. It gleamed in the pink light from the desk lamp, wet with his precum. It was a short dick but nicely shaped; I would have sucked it gladly. He aimed it at her cunt and just slid it in, then out again. He began ramming her with it and she started to bite my cock. I tried pulling away again but Joe held me. Tina tried to develop a rhythm but Jeffrey's plowing was erratic. For somebody who was so into fucking, I didn't think he was very good. Maybe he'd had some of Joe's pills; I didn't know and it didn't really matter because I could feel Joe's hard-on rubbing against the cheeks of my ass. Was this the way he wanted it? To do it to me while his friend did it to the girl, to somehow be linked? I didn't have a clue but her teeth were killing me and I took her head and steadied it, then tried drawing it back but every time I did, Jeffrey would ram her again. Joe was pulling my pants down the rest of the way. Then he pulled my shoes off and I was soon naked from the waist down. Finally, Tina came up for air and I yanked myself away. Joe stepped into my place and Tina unzipped his pants and his cock flopped out; it was only semi-hard. She kissed it, then played with his balls. I went around him and held him as he had held me, my erection sliding between the cheeks of his ass. I lowered his pants just enough so that skin would touch skin.

"Look at him go," Joe sighed as Jeffrey grabbed Tina's ass and really let her have it. He pulled all the way out then rammed it in to the hilt, then back out. "Music is rhythm and so is sex," Joe had said, "and Jeffrey has the best rhythm of anybody I've ever seen." I watched now as Jeffrey fucked and tried to get into his rhythm; it was too fast for me, too furious, like all he meant to do was hurt, but I almost had it when suddenly he asked, "Hey, you like pussy, don't you Willy? You gotta have some of this."

He lifted his leg over the bench and stood there, massaging his prick. It really gleamed now, dripping wet with her cunt juice. I didn't want to fuck her; I really wanted him to bring that cock over to my mouth and let me suck it, wet with Tina's juice and all, I didn't care, I just wanted to suck it, but for Joe's sake I wanted to play the game. "Joe first," I said, teasing him.

"Yeah, I'll take over there," Jeffrey said. Watching Tina devour Jeffrey's cock, I suddenly felt left out, wondering why I was there at all. I wondered how often they had done this to a girl. It seemed so natural for them, one at one end, one at the other. But Joe's cock was still limp. As he had done with me the night before, he got the head of it in but it was no use, he just couldn't fuck. I thought of all the nights, all the days when he had been hard and had come like there was no tomorrow while I was fucking him. I knew where his heart was and it wasn't in fucking this cunt. I wanted to fuck him right then but I held back. I waited for his move.

"You'd better do it, little stud," he said to me, "you and Jeffrey, fuck the hell out of her."

"In bed," Jeffrey said, pulling his cock away from Tina's mouth and having her stand up. We followed him into the bedroom. He handed me a tube of grease and then laid down on the bed on his back. He told Tina to get on her knees and squat on his prick.

"Hmmmm," she groaned as she guided it in.

I greased my cock and then her ass and got on the bed behind her. Soon we were rocking together on the waterbed, fucking her together. Joe completely undressed and stood on the bed, lowering his limp dick into her mouth. He fucked her mouth with it while she raised and lowered herself over our pricks. She moaned and groaned, going crazy with it.

Watching us below him turned Joe on and eventually his cock was almost hard. Suddenly, he knelt on the bed next to me, watching as the girl moved up and down on our cocks, Jeffrey playing with her tits, squeezing them, sucking on them. Joe put his left arm around me and with his right hand jacked off until he had a dry orgasm. I couldn't help it, I hugged him, then kissed him, then pulled out of her and told him we were going back to the hotel. He put up no resistance.

Joe dozed off in the limo on the way back to the Plaza. I struggled to get him up the steps to the lobby but then one of the bellmen helped me. We finally got him to the door of the suite, then I took over. The effects of the pill he'd given me had worn off and, after running the whole scene over in my mind while we were riding back, I made up my mind how I was going to end the night: deep inside Joe Skinner's ass.

When I went into the suite and switched on the lights, I heard voices, then, nothing. I helped Joe into our bedroom and pushed him onto the bed. Then I went down the hall and found Benny's door open. He was sitting in bed alone, naked, sipping a cocktail. I heard the toilet flush in the bathroom.

"Just in time for the party," he said, slurring his words.

Not another drunk, I thought. I shook my head and had the door knob in my hand when the bathroom door opened and a man stepped out. In the dim light it was hard to see how old he was but he was no kid., maybe in his early 30's. He had muscles for days but an angry look about him, as if I was competition showing up at the last minute. "Yeah?" he said.

"Just sayin' goodnight to Benny," I said and continued to close the door.

"Catch ya later," he said.

I hope not, I thought.

I locked the door to our bedroom behind me and got undressed. I stripped Joe and got him on his stomach. I parted his ass and laid my cock between the cheeks. I was so horny I didn't need to penetrate him; just watching myself in the mirror, I rolled over his body and I came. If he'd been awake, he'd have loved it.

*

The next morning, Joe hung up the phone and said, "My folks got back from Europe over the weekend."

"Are we going to see them?" I was stuffing my souvenirs in the new Hartmann suitcase Benny bought for me.

Joe chuckled. "No, but we won't be able to take the jet back to L.A.. We'll have to fly commercial."

"Commercial?"

I had never ridden on any plane before the corporate jet, but I'd seen them sitting on the runway. That was really as close as I wanted to get but then he said, "Well, not really. You'll see."

The MGM shuttle left from Kennedy airport and Joe was the only celebrity on the flight so we got more attention than anybody else. He said, "These flights are great fun, kid. Once Dolly Parton and I sang happy birthday to Ernest Borgnine. Shit, you never know who you're gonna to meet." Leaning back in the big lounge chair, I wondered what flying on a regular plane would be like. We sat there for the longest time together comfortably in silence, like longtime companions, watching the City across the wing as we sailed by it.

The stewards were falling all over themselves to wait on us but Joe didn't have a drink. He knew he had to be in front of the cameras the next day. "Yeah I drink," he said to the steward. "If I'm happy, I'm a happy drunk. If I'm somebody else, I'm a something-else drunk. But my drinking now is very intermittent. Like, I'll have a little something four days a week and then every once in a while, I'll binge. Shit, man, I used to binge for years."

"Yeah, I know" I said as the guy left.

"But then, one time at 7:30 in the morning I had a joint in one hand and a bourbon in the other - "

"Whose joint?"

He laughed. "Not whose, it."

"Oh."

"Anyway, I decided I wasn't gonna drink any more until five o'clock."

"It's five o'clock in New York now." My beer was gone. I needed another. I wondered where the steward had gone.

Joe leaned back in his seat, closed his eyes. "Yeah, it's all on page 449."

"What?"

"In the AA book. I'll never forget it, on page 449." He opened his eyes again and became very animated. "It says you're in the place you're supposed to be. What I'm doin' now is trying to create a whole new thing. Instead of the group it's just me and I wanted to bring my vocal out of the mix, to unclutter the arrangements, get a certain focus into it, yet cover the whole terrain. You know, a collection of highs and lows."

"I love it." I wondered how many times I was going to have to tell him how much I loved the new album. Because it hadn't "gone gold" yet, it was as if he had to be reassured every five minutes he was doing the right thing. "It's wonderful, man. Better than Randy Travis."

He chuckled. "That's important to me, to hear you say that. That's the nicest compliment you've ever paid me." He put his hand on top of mine. "Well, almost. You know, at this point, everything I do has to be important. I may be dying, for chrissakes."

"Oh?" Now he was back to dying again. I felt like saying, Give me some air, but I didn't.

"You never know these days, kid. But anyway, maybe what I tried to do wasn't that well received but I've gotta try, you know?"

"Yeah," I said as he rubbed the back of my hand. I closed my own eyes and could hardly wait to get home because there was only one sure way to get him to stop doubting himself, to stop talking, and that was with my dick in his mouth.

From the LP "I Remember You"/Sung by Joe Skinner/Side 2, Cut 4:
"More Than You Know:" "I've been looking for you / Where did you go?
...Everybody says I'm wasting my time / I must reply, the time I waste is
certainly mine."

When we returned to the special field where MGM lands, Harold met us with the limo. We dropped Benny off at his place in Brentwood, then went home.

I was exhausted but Joe had to have a soak. And, of course, as it always did with Joe, one thing led to another. He could never get enough.

And while I was watching in the mirrors as I fucked him, I realized how much I'd missed being at the house, having this routine. But even with the production being way over schedule there were now less than two weeks on the shoot at Disney. Then what? The next morning, I was determined to find out.

I had all this stuff in the computer, what was I going to do with it? Somebody would have to sort it all out, make sense of it, put it in order. As Joe was having his coffee and rolls I brought the box of computer discs into the kitchen.

"...What am I supposed to do with all these files?" I asked him.

"I've been thinking about that. I want to hire a ghostwriter and have you work with him. You might learn something. I know a guy, a screenwriter, that's great and he's available. It should be done like a movie, don't you think?"

"Yeah, I guess. Who is it?"

"His name is Rodney Templeton...oh, but he's got a problem."

"Oh?"

"Yeah, he's gay. Openly gay, I mean. Would you object to a gay guy?"

"No." I looked down at my feet.

"I would. He couldn't keep his hands to himself."

"I'd smack 'im."

"Ha! This guy you probably would. But he'd keep on trying."

Let 'im try," I said, raising my arm in a punch.

"Good kid." He kissed me goodbye. Harold was waiting in the drive with the motor running.

*

"I have a terrible sex drive," Rodney said as we were reading over an anecdote Joe had told me about a typical night on the road.

"Terrible? How?" I asked.

"Can't get enough."

"Shit, everybody has that problem."

"Except Joe Skinner. It sounds like he gets all he wants."

"Not anymore."

"You mean you play hard to get?"

"Sometimes, when I want something."

He laughed. Laughed so hard his belly shook. Joe was right, he was obnoxious, but he was very smart and taught me a lot. "Structure," he said. "You got to put all this in some kind of structure. Chapters, sub-chapters. Then we'll work with it. I don't think we need to put everything in exact chronological order. We should group it, though. There are so many things going on at the same time."

I'd sit at the desk with him as he'd edit the stories, pouring over the material, hour after hour, reading it right off the computer screen. I added what I could but it was his show now. I didn't want my part to be over, though. Not just yet. So I stuck close to him. Maybe too close.

"...God, you are beautiful," he said at one point, turning from the screen and looking at me as I came into the room carrying a beer for him.

"Thanks."

"But it's odd, there's an earthy quality about you that -well, it's like you're rough, but gentle at the same time - "

"Like a farmboy?"

"Exactly. In a way you remind me of that guy on the Waltons, Richard Thomas. Not in looks, really, but in manner."

"He's an old man now, isn't he?"

"I'm sure he'd love to hear that!"

"Ever sleep with him?"

"No. And if I had he wouldn't have gotten much sleep."

Later, he asked: "...Do you have any friends your own age?"

"No. Not here. Not anywhere, really. I just came out here from Ohio."

"I was hoping you might have some friends who like to play around, some friends as cute as you are."

"Not a one."

"That's a shame. There should be more like you."

"No, one like me's plenty, believe me."

"Then if there's only one, it should be spread around."

"But I'm spoken for. But, look, I know some people, maybe I could find something for you."

"I'd appreciate all the help you can give me."

And it went on like that, day after day. It grew old fast. I ran out of ways to say no but I wasn't about to call Van. No way.

"Look," I said in the second week, "I'm going shopping; Harold's taking me." And we left. I was determined to find somebody for Rodney. He seemed nice but proud, as if he wasn't about to pay for it. So I figured I'd give him a little present, but I couldn't bring it to the house. Joe wouldn't hear of it. So I decided to buy somebody and stick 'em at the Econo Lodge and have Rodney go there. That was the plan. I made up a story that Joe wanted Harold to take the Chevy in for service. He'd done that before so it was no big deal, but I wanted to ride along. Get away from Rodney. That Harold could understand. So we took off, the chauffeur and the live-in stud in the old Chevy with the top down. It was a trip. I put on my new Ray-Bans just like Joe's and acted the part. Harold, who usually showed no emotion at all, laughed like hell.

We cruised the boulevard but I decided Rodney needed something better than street trash. No way was I going to get into a bar, though. I had no drivers license, no fake ID. We decided to just sit in the car and wait near The Pink Elephant. It didn't take long.

He was black. Rodney had mentioned he liked 'em dark. I figured that meant really dark. He said his name was Slick. Harold got out of the car to get cigarettes while I talked to the dude.

"So, what's up?" he asked. He was dressed like a businessman, without a tie. Neat, clean, almost elegant. Lots of gold jewelry.

"You a cop?"

"No. You one?"

"Hardly."

"Who's that?" he asked, pointing to Harold walking across the street.

"My chauffeur."

"Yeah, okay," he chuckled. "So then, what's up?"

"A party."

"Yeah? Where?"

"Econo Lodge up on Vine."

"I know it. When?"

"Eight. Say eight. There'll be a red Cadillac parked in front of the door."

And it went on like that. I told him I had a friend in from out of town who was a real closet case and he needed a good drilling.

"Okay. How much?"

We agreed on $150. I gave him $50 as a down payment.

*

The next morning, Benny came to the house around nine o'clock. Matty hadn't arrived yet. "We need to talk," he said. He looked awful.

"What's wrong?"

"How could you?"

"How could I what?"

"Set up Rodney like that?"

"What happened?"

"He was beaten and robbed last night, that's what happened."

"Shit."

"I was just at the hospital. He did you a favor, you know. He didn't have them call Joe, he had them call me."

My pa was right. I wasn't just dumb. "I'm so fuckin' stupid!" I screamed.

"You meant no harm; we both understand that. Rodney agreed to it. You take a chance, no matter what. But if Joe finds out -"

"I didn't think. I should've just let well enough alone."

"If you wanted to please him, you should have done the job yourself. That's your business, isn't it?"

"I retired, remember?"

"I hadn't noticed."

I walked away from him, out onto the balcony. I thought of jumping off to get away from him.

Soon he was standing behind me. "Why don't we just keep this as a secret between the three of us."

"Anything you say."

He clamped his hand on my crotch. "It's better that way, kid."

"That's what it comes down to, then?"

"Yes. And I won't hurt you. I just want to make love to you."

I gripped the railing. It was bound to happen, one way or another, I realized. They always get what they want. They have the power. What was I after all, but just a kid? And a kid from a farm in Ohio, for chrissakes.

He slid the robe down off my shoulder and kissed my skin.

"Matty's due any minute," I said, moving away from him, going down the steps. "Let's go to my room."

...I closed my eyes as his mouth clamped around my limp cock. I hadn't even taken my shower and I was sure it still smelled of the coat of cum from the night before, but that probably turned him on even more. He worked it over and I kept thinking about Joe. As long as he didn't know, know about how stupid I was, know what I had to do to stay here, maybe it was all right. I had to allow myself to let somebody do this. I had grown to respect Mr. Kaplan. And, as he worked it over in his mouth, I realized he was a good cocksucker. It could have been worse.

My cock finally rose to meet his lips and he really started to get on it. "Yeah, that's more like it," he cried, and he slid down onto his knees. Poor little man was worshipping my cock.

I remembered the rough trade in his room at the Plaza and I decided if I had to do this, I was going to have some fun with it. I began slapping his face with my cock, forcing it between his lips, into his throat. He really got off on that, cumming right away. But he didn't want it to end. He held my ass and cried, "Fuck my mouth, kid. Fuck my fuckin' mouth with that big thing." I thought, better than your ass, and I let him have it.

He was so good, I started cumming. I pulled out and he hugged me. I shot my load all over the top of his head. He cried, "Oh, no," and reached up, running his fingers through the stickiness.

"Sorry, but you can get it cleaned."

He laughed, then lifted the toupee from his scalp and threw it across the room. He pushed me back against the wall and started sucking it again, my cock, slick with cum, sliding between his lips and back down his throat.

Seizing me that way, wanting more after I'd already given everything, jolted me and suddenly, something snapped. I wanted to be mean to him. I grabbed him by the ears and forced his head back and forth the full length of my cock. The head of it popped from his mouth and it began to harden again. I kept yanking his head back and forth and the more I did, the more he seemed to love it. I didn't expect that. I wanted him to hate it, to feel some pain with this. I was now feeling terrible pain, that I'd let Joe down, let myself down. I'd been stupid. I wanted to ram my cock so far down Benny's throat that he gagged on it. I shoved him, pushing him onto his back and when he hit the floor I pounced on his chest, taking my hardon and jamming it in his mouth. I held the back of his head and began face-fucking him with a fury that I couldn't believe. This wasn't sex anymore, this was punishment. I was punishing him but also punishing myself. He bit my cock a couple of times and I slapped him on either side of the head. He began to kick his legs and his arms twisted my shoulders. He tried to pull my cock out of his mouth but it was no use, I had him pinned. And then I came again. Cum flowed down his throat and he fought harder than ever, but I wouldn't release him. Soon all the wind had been drained from him and I stood up. He lay there on the floor in the big mirrored bedroom and began to cry. "I hope to God you're not sick. I swallowed it. I swallowed it."

"I'm not sick," I said, stepping away from him, heading for the bathroom. I felt like saying I wasn't the sick one here but I didn't.

A few moments later, while I was washing my cock at the sink in Joe's black marble bathroom, Benny came in and stood behind me.

"You sure can surprise a person." He ran his hands up and down my body and brought them to rest on my balls. He kissed my shoulder. "We'll just keep this a secret between us, okay?"

I nodded but I had made up my mind that somehow I was going to find the courage to tell Joe I'd been an asshole.

*

"...The bitch is on 'Current Affair,'" Joe yelled as he came through the door.

He grabbed the remote and started scanning the channels. It was just a little after seven. The show had already started. It was the last segment so they kept mentioning it all through the other stuff about a man who murdered his wife and a son who murdered his mother.

After the show, while we ate the dinner Matty had left, he told me all about the case: "Don't worry, kid, I got my attorneys working on it right now. She'll be sorry she ever started this shit. I finally remembered. She was there the first night we played Indianapolis. She was in the room with us for a while. You know, Paulie doing his own thing, watching me. But then Luisa was coming in and I left. I never saw her again. Paulie didn't OD until two nights later, our last night there. Like I say, I've been studying all the aspects of this shit while I've been at the studio and I've been on the phone with my attorneys. The law's on our side. I know the law, kid. You know, I've always been fascinated by the law. I wanted to be a lawyer. When I was a kid, I thought F. Lee Bailey was the greatest thing there ever was. I read 'The Defense Never Rests' and his other book and I was really into it. I'd act out courtroom scenes in my father's office. His office is as big as a courthouse, for chrissakes.

"But I found out I had to have these great fuckin' grades to get into law school so then I decided I wanted to sing. I'd sung in the choir; I'd sung for my girlfriends. I sang in the shower. I sang all the time. I was like always on, so why not get paid for it? I got a lot of inspiration from the saloon singers, Tony Bennett, Sinatra, Mel Torme. I wanted to be romantic like that but I wasn't going to get anywhere with that gig in the seventies. So when Jeffrey asked me to join his band and sing, I dug it. Hell, they even changed the name because of me. Paulie came up with it. He said it was like when we chose up sides for basketball at school; one was shirts, the other was skins, and we were always skins and we so we decided with me as the singer that's what we'd be. And of course we couldn't wear shirts. That's when I went to the gym. I wanted to look better than any of the other guys with my shirt off. Well, I was supposed to. Shit, I was upfront."

"Yeah, you were upfront all right," I laughed, groping him, then clearing the table.

"That's all you ever think about, isn't it?"

"Beats feelin' sorry for myself."

"Yeah, what you got to feel sorry about?" He came up behind me at the sink.

I kissed him. "Nothin'. Right now, absolutely nothin'."

*

"Rodney's in the hospital," I told Joe after we'd fucked. I was washing myself in the bathroom; he was lying in bed, recovering.
"Oh?"
"Yeah. Nothin' serious. He just picked the wrong trick. But I want to go see him tomorrow, okay?"
"I'll have Harold come back and take you."
I walked back into the room. "I'm afraid it's going to slow up the book."
"Yeah, well, maybe we'll get away for a while."
"Serious?"
"Yeah. When they wrap the movie we'll go to Maui. You know I bought a condo over there from Jim Nabors and I've never even seen it?"
"I'd love it."
"But that's for later and we'll spend at least a week. Now, we'll just take another long weekend. They're even further behind schedule on the picture but they won't need me till Wednesday. What do you say we leave Saturday?"
"Leave for where?"
"The mountains."
"Which mountains?"
"Near Lake Arrowhead. I haven't been there since that time with Jeffrey and Luisa."
"And you want to go back?"
"Sure. Now. I've never wanted to go back till now."
"Well, okay, but on one condition."
"What's that?"
"That we do everything."
"You back on that shit again? I told you, if I wanted a woman I'd get one."
"I know, but just once...in the mountains."
"Well, I'll think about it. You be nice to me and I'll keep thinking about it." And he rolled over, exposing his ass to me again, moving his hips, wanting it. It seemed he could never get enough of my cock. It was enough for him, but it wasn't enough for me. I had to know what it would be like with him on top. Just once.

*

"I'm so sorry," I told Rodney. I'd brought him flowers. "Orchids," the saleslady said. "He'll love it," I said.

"It wasn't your fault, kid."

"But it was. I shoulda known better."

"It was me. I've let Joe down. I feel terrible."

"He said there's plenty of time. We're going to the mountains this weekend anyway, so when you get out, we'll start right back up again."

"Taking you to the mountains, eh? God, Joe must love having you around."

"Yeah, I'm sorta like a human dildo. Yeah, that's it, the human dildo. The dildo was a dodo."

"Don't be so hard on yourself. You've come a long way in a short while."

And I realized he was right. I closed my eyes and remembered what I'd told Joe, "I'm a fool for just about anything. Once some guy called me gullible. I guess that's what I am, totally gullible. If I'm told something I believe it until it's proved otherwise. I always wanted to believe people. I still do.

"Yeah, most of the guys I met on the street, they had hope for the future. Like the white knight was going to show up. They thought I was a joke at first. They wondered how I ever found my way home."

Now I had a home, well, sort of a home, but I couldn't forget what Luisa had said, that the bed would turn cold. I wasn't prepared for that. I needed to get my shit together. "I appreciate your not being mad at me," I told Rodney. "I'll make it up to you, I promise."

He didn't say anything for several moments, just stared at me. Then he said, "Sure. If you say so."

"Well, ya never know."

"No, kid, you never know."

From the LP "I Remember You" / Sung by Joe Skinner / Side 2, Cut 5, "Let's Get Lost:" "Let's get lost / Lost in each other's arms / Let's get lost / Let them send out alarms / Although they'll think us rather rude / Let's defrost in a romantic mist / Let's get crossed off everybody's list / To celebrate this time we found each other / Oh, kid, let's get lost."

We left in the morning, the top down, Joe's eyes hidden behind tinted glass.

When I slipped on my own new Ray-Bans, Joe laughed, "Yeah, the Hollywood kid."

Eventually we got off the freeway in San Bernadino and stopped at an Italian place, Bon Appetito, and had red wine with lunch.

He handed me a passbook. It had my name on the first page.

"You gotta have a bank account in L.A. You don't want to live like a pigeon."

"But I've got no money."

"Now you do."

I looked down at the first page. The balance was $1,000. "Wow," I sighed.

"Hey, kid, you deserve it. I'd become a real loner. I didn't intend for that to happen but it did. I didn't realize just how lonely I was until you came along. And to know sex the way a woman knows it, to have that power in my asshole, to know both sides the way Paulie did, well, you did it."

"I'm glad." I felt like continuing, that I wanted to feel that, too, if only he'd let me, but I didn't. I knew he would, once we got to the mountains.

"Yeah, I wasn't taking care of business for a long time, kid. Now I want to do this tour. I need Jeffrey on keyboard and I want you with me, to stay with me, to stay on the road with me."

I drew a deep breath, a breath of relief.

"Yeah, Eddie Van Halen has Valerie, I want my William."

"I'm glad."

"Oh, they do well, Valerie and Eddie. She comes in and stays a while, keeps him happy. That's what I needed, somebody like that." He chuckled. "Yeah, Eddie's world revolves around himself and he married himself. They're very happy with each other."

"I'm very happy with you."

"I'm happy too, almost as happy as I was when I was a kid. See, I had to invent everything I am as I went along. I created my own little fantasy world when I was a kid, populated it with characters, and it all came true. Except the women. I never really understood why but I guess I just don't really like women." He sighed. "Oh, well, now it's one big party thrown by God in our honor."

He went on about his plans for the tour. It would be different, completely different from the rock tour: "... We visualized what the kids were hearing. It was a complete experience. The minute you heard our songs you visualized what it looked like, what it represented, how it talked, how it walked. And we gave it to 'em. Now, I'm going to make it intimate, even if it's a big hall. It'll just be me and Jeffrey. Shit, I may even sit on a stool like Sinatra does."

"And you want me to tag along?"

"You bet. See, it was difficult bein' on the road. You don't make friends on the road; you just have all these people around you telling you how great you are all the time. Nobody is there to spank you."

I chuckled. "Yeah, I'll spank you all right."

"Shit, spoil me's what you do."

"No, I'm the one that's spoiled." I rubbed the cover of the passbook.

"Well, I look at it this way, you don't meet all kinds of people, just some kinds of people. You're the kind I want on the road."

We ordered another bottle of wine and he went on: "God, it was insane being on the road. I'd never do it again, like that, if I had a band. The Stones, they do it right, maybe three months every two or three years. That's the formula. You get to be saturated and people say, 'Oh, I missed them but I'll catch them next year.' It's no longer an event. Yeah, this'll be an event, only twelve cities, me and Jeffrey together again. Yeah, it'll be great." He beamed. "Hey, maybe we'll even get some mean pussy along the way, like we had in New York. What do you think?"

It was the first time he had spoken of New York. I wasn't sure he'd even remembered. I didn't know what to think, just sipped my wine.

"I loved it, you know," he said.

"Loved what?"

"Watching that gorgeous big dick of yours going in and out of that cunt. You were everything I told Jeffrey you'd be and more. Shit, he still talks about you." He thought a moment. "I think he'd like let to get it on with you. But you're mine, not his, remember that."

"How could I forget?" I slipped the passbook in the back pocket of my jeans and smiled.

When we finally left, I was high on the wine and the excitement of what was to come, his acceptance of my being part of his life for a while longer, his acceptance of my need to know the way a woman feels the same as he did. And, as we climbed higher into the mountains it got colder and, after he put the top up, I snuggled against him.

As the rich gold of the trees sailed by us, I put his new LP on the stereo, then unzipped his pants. I took his cock out and played with it until it was almost hard, then went down on it. Every time I would get him close, he'd start weaving on the curvy road and almost run us into the forest.

When we left the main road, the sun was setting and we were suddenly into thick clouds. The road zigzagged upwards, with shoulders that ended at the pine forest. The air was dry, filled with the smell of pine and what Joe said was eucalyptus. The effect of the wine was slowly wearing off but now I was drunk with other things, with the smells, the sounds and the taste of Joe's cock. I didn't want him to come but finally he just couldn't help it and when he was finished, Lake Arrowhead was in front of us.

We drove around to the south edge where the cabins were, past the piers with small boats tied up, and the water was shining, dancing in the moonlight. We got out of the car and I hugged him.

"Tonight's the night," he teased, squeezing my ass.

I could hardly wait to get undressed.

*

He made the cozy rooms even cozier. It seemed he was celebrating the taking of my cherry, getting off on it more than I was. He lighted candles in the living room and the bedroom. "This is the honeymoon suite," he kidded me when he were carrying our suitcases in.

"Only one with mirrors, I'll bet," I said.

Now he brought out a joint. "I've been saving this," he said. "I don't mess with this shit anymore but tonight, well, tonight, I think you'll need this."

I didn't argue. Anything was better than his going to the bottle of Jack Daniels he'd packed. "I wish we had some of the great stuff Johnny used to get but..." He hesitated, thinking. "Yeah, there was always a history to every drug, like the hash from Turkey, the grass from Jamaica, the LSD from up north, a chemist he knew. Now, the hashish, that I could handle. It's a good thing to try. We'll do it one day. Once you make it a habit, though, I understand the boundaries begin to contract again. But there's a point when the limits vanish, the limits between reality and what isn't quite real, I mean. You perceive reality as something that might be happening inside you or outside you." He shook his head. "It's hard to explain if you haven't tried it. I just know you feel things more deeply than before, or you feel other things, other kinds of things. It's qualitative more than quantitative. But, oh God, the LSD! Did I ever tell you about the first time I did that?"

I shook my head and knew we were off on another story I would have to remember when I got back to my computer at the house. "See, Johnny was the one that was into all the exotic stuff and one night we were just hangin' out at the beach house he and Jeffrey had rented in Malibu and he got into the mind-expanding benefits of LSD. This guy could go on for hours about it. I could only imagine it. I told him that's all I wanted to do, just imagine it, but he insisted I try it. He handed me a small paper stamp and told me to swallow it. In just a few minutes I began to feel different. It was as if something had a hold of my shoulders, grabbing me, and then everything got fuzzy, like you say happens to you on grass. He told me later that I stood up and walked over to the windows and looked out at the Ocean. I just stood there. Finally, I started reacting to the rhythm of one of our songs that he'd put on the stereo. I went over to the piano where Jeffrey always practiced and started to play. But the white keys looked like they were fused together. I tried to play and only one finger would work. I ran from the house, out onto the beach and there was a man walking along with his dog. I don't know why but I thought he was God, coming to take me away. I scared the shit out of him and he called the cops. By the time they got there, I was asleep. They'd made so many calls to that house that they took it as another of our harmless disturbances. But it was funny, Johnny said that they warned him that if he didn't mend his ways - " A sadness suddenly entered his eyes. He shook his head and lit the joint. He took a toot and handed it to me. "Good stuff. Better than we used to get in the old days.

"But, anyhow, the next day was a killer. I couldn't remember the trip, I was in a panic all day. It was frightening. It scared the shit outta me. But it helped me understand Johnny. Why what happened, happened."

I nodded and handed the joint back to him. We didn't say anything for a long while, just letting the drug sweep over us.

Finally, he smiled. "They should legalize drugs, then there wouldn't be so many murders. But it's all so corrupt. I think they want to keep the people down and drugs is the best thing to do that. And it's the only way they make any money and then they get caught so then we have to build more prisons. That's all we're gonna have is prisons. One big fuckin' prison. Give me the old days, man. When we were doing it, it was almost innocent." He chuckled. "Speaking of innocent, bring your sweet virgin ass over here."

He was sitting in the largest chair in the living room and I got up from the couch and slid into his lap. Our hands seemed to automatically go to each other's cocks. Our lips met and I brought my other hand to his face. I wanted to tell him I loved him but I was afraid. Instead I just let him keep on kissing me. Finally, he asked, "You ready?"

I thought about saying, Who wouldn't be?, but I didn't. I just stood up and let him lead me into the bedroom

From the LP "I Remember You"/Sung by Joe Skinner/Side 2, Cut 6, "A
Time for Love:" "...A time for holding hands together / A time for rainbow
colored weather / A time for that make believe that we've been dreaming
of / As time goes drifting by / The willow bends and so do I / But oh my
friends/ Whatever sky above / I'm sure, a time for spring/ A time for fall
/ But most of all, a time for love."

Joe pulled me tightly to his chest and I felt his prick quiver and
harden against mine. He kissed my lips and I offered no resistance
as he began shoving his tongue deep into my mouth. He continued
shoving, then withdrawing, as if he was fucking me with it. As he
withdrew his tongue, I whispered, "I want you." And soon I was
flat on my stomach and he was massaging me, then he started
slipping his fingers in my ass.

"You greased yourself," he chuckled.

"No, that's cum left from the last customer."

He slapped my asscheeks, first one side, then the other. "Dirty
slut." He kept slapping them. It was beginning to hurt. Suddenly
he stopped and began kissing them, sucking them, making a fuss
over them. "Your ass is almost as nice as mine," he said.

"Better. I'm a virgin."

With that he shoved in three fingers and I screamed. He loved it.
Four fingers, screwing me. I screamed again. He pulled them out
and went back to kissing my ass, holding the cheeks up, shoving
his tongue inside me, playing with my cock while he did.

After a few minutes, he rolled me over and got on his knees over
my face. The blue veins of his cock strained against the skin of his
prick, stretching up as his hand moved rapidly over it. He pulled
the head of my cock with the tips of his lips, then opened his mouth
and began licking it, savoring the sweet taste of my prick. The
moonlight filtered through the window and blended with the glow
of the candle. The beat of the music, not a Skins CD but Robert
Palmer, one of his favorites, pounded in my head. The pot had its
effect; it felt as if I was floating on the bed.

Slowly I moved up and down over his cock, circling the top and flicking my tongue around its head as he groaned. We stayed in the 69 position for several minutes, then he rolled over on his side and as he played with my cock with one hand with his other hand he was squeezing and pinching my nipples.

I suddenly raised my hips and brought one leg over his body and straddled him. I guided the elegant tool into my ass and sat back, feeling the hugeness of him fill me as my muscles grasped it and tightened around it. Slowly, slowly I raised myself until, when I looked behind me, I could see all but the tip of it, then I slid down on it again, and began riding him as he so often rode me. I bent forward and he took my pecs in his hands and squeezed them and began kissing me. I was drowning in his spit as he kissed every inch of my face.

As he raised me up and held my shoulders, then shoved upward, jabbing, stabbing me, my head bent forward, my hair covering his face, and I stifled a scream of pain by biting his shoulder. He rolled me over again and pushed me down on the bed and took me as I had taken him when I felt he wanted it that way. He cradled me in his arms and told me he would be gentle. I could feel him guiding his cock with his hand, increasing the pressure to get the head past my tight opening. Then came the most difficult part, his cock growing wider and wider toward the base. But he was easy with it. Suddenly, my resistance was gone. Soon the base of his cock was tight against me, completely in me, then he started moving, slowly, rhythmically, in and out. One hand and arm were under my neck, holding my shoulder, the other hand moved up to grab my balls and then my cock. I met every thrust. I contracted, sucked, squeezed, and held his cock with every stroke, then hung on as he pulled back.

He took my cock in his hands and pumped it. I didn't want to come but I couldn't help myself. I clamped my hands on his gorgeous ass and pushed it so that all of him was in me. "Oh, shit," I groaned as my cum splattered everywhere. He took my head in his hands and held it steady, then kissed me. Soon I could feel his own cum entering me. I didn't want him to wear a rubber. I had bought some spermacide at the drugstore and prepared myself so that I could take it the way it was meant to be and was glad I did. I remembered what that girl had said at Jeffrey's, something about essence, and now I had the essence of Joe exploding in me.

"Yes, yes," I cried, slapping his ass.

He rolled on his side and brought me with him. We laid there, holding each other, with his cock still in me, for several minutes and then he started again, with little movements at first, then stronger. I ground myself up against him and, crazy with it, I cried, "Oh, Joe, I love it. I love you!"

I'd never told anybody that before.

"I love you, too, kid. I really do." And then he came again, more of his essence filling me, as he jacked me off.

*

Sunday we hiked and found a place where we could get naked and it was as if he had discovered a new toy. "You're so damn tight," he said, thrusting his fingers into me before he shoved his cock in.

"See what you've been missing," I said, saying it more to myself than to him. Feeling his cock fill me turned me on like nothing ever had. And having him get off on it like he did made it even more exciting. He fucked me in the woods, then fucked me in the shower when we got back to the cabin. It was as if I was with someone completely different and I thought maybe, just maybe, he would want to keep me around a little while longer.

"...We haven't talked much about your life," he said while I unwrapped the basket of food Matty had made for us.

"Not much to tell."

"It must have been terrible, that's why I've never pushed it."

"It was," I said, opening the bottle of wine. "But you've made up for every minute of it, believe me."

"Having to go with people just for the money - "

"Oh, you meant that part of my life. Well, that really wasn't me. It was like the easiest thing for me to do when I got here. Hell, I was even met at the bus!" I munched my triple decker sandwich. "But I knew you'd get around to asking about it sooner or later. The answer is: sometimes. Sometimes I enjoyed it. Mostly not. And sometimes I hated it. Okay?"

"Okay? Okay, what?"

"Okay, do you know enough? Can we just forget about it?"

"I'll let it go, forever, if you will."

"All right," I said, pouring some wine. "All right."

The next morning, Joe was watching me busy myself making breakfast and he said, "You're a helluva kid, you know that?"

"Thanks."

"What I said about loving you, it's true. I really think I do love you. And I haven't said that very often in my life."

I didn't turn around and look at him, I just kept buttering the toast. "I love you, too," I mumbled. "And I've never said that to anybody."

"Never?"

"Never."

He chuckled, as if he was savoring a victory of some kind. "Well, now that we love each other, we have to help each other."

"Nobody's helped me like you have, Joe. I can read, I got a bank account -"

He interrupted me. "Hey, kid, you deserve everything you get. And now I want your help."

"Anything." I went over to the stove to check on the eggs.

"Well, I never told you this but Luisa had a kid. My kid."

"Oh?"

"Yeah. Didn't tell me. She told me she had an abortion, but I found out she didn't. She put the kid up for adoption. A girl." He paused, thinking, then went on, sadly, "God, I hope she's not having to put up with what I had to put up with. I remember when I was just getting known and these stories about the road began to appear. I went home and Daddy says to me, 'You got a smug look, you know that: your face sickens me. You've become scum and I'm tired of scum.' Can you imagine?"

I shook my head. "I can't believe fathers can be so cruel."

He came over to the stove and ran his hands up my back.

"That's why I want to find her. To help. Not to mess up her life. I don't know what her life is but it's important to me to know. She's somewhere in Georgia. I'll find her one day. I want you to help me."

"I will. I'll find her for you."

"You know, one time Luisa went so far as to come up with a death certificate, trying to tell me the baby had died. But I found out that was a lie. She was just trying to protect the kid. But it hurt me that she'd do that. But what's done is done. Now I'd just like to know, you know, that's she's okay."

"Should we put it in the book?"

"Yeah," he said, kissing me on the back of the neck. "That's the end of the book. You and I go off looking for my daughter."

We embraced and I said, "Great ending, Joe, great ending."

From the LP "I Remember You"/Sung by Joe Skinner/Side 2, Cut 7, "Don't Explain:" "Hush, now, don't explain / I know you've raised Cain...Quiet, don't explain / You're my joy and pain / I'm glad you're bad / Don't explain."

Joe started drinking wine with dinner and never stopped. Then he began reading the words Rodney had written so far. He had brought the computer printout with him. Finally he said, "This shit's good."

"And he's got all those pictures picked out, too." I started to leaf through them, admiring how handsome Joe was no matter how long his hair was, no matter what age he was.

"Pictures. You always fall back on pictures, don't you?" he said, with an anger that frightened me.

I smiled. "Oh, no, they're not for me, they're for your fans."

"Yeah, I wish I could tell my fans the whole truth. Still, he'd better call it an 'unauthorized biography,' it'll sell better." Suddenly he slammed down his wine glass, "Shit, what's this?"

"What?"

"He's got some shit in here about my not playing AIDS benefits because I don't want to be identified with gays. Where'd that come from?"

"Well - "

"Look, I'm always interested in the way people speak and what they speak about, but I don't identify with any causes. I don't want them putting something between them and the act, you know? Like with Jane Fonda, it's either this exercise guru or it's Hanoi Jane. It gets in the way. And the last fuckin' thing I need is to be identified with gays, AIDS or no AIDS." His voice trailed away. He saw I was suddenly sad. "Is that wrong?"

"No. It's just that, here we are - "

"Look, what we do here is nobody's business. I don't need to take a billboard on Sunset just to tell them we fuck, do I?"

"No. But it wouldn't hurt to do a benefit. Everybody does a benefit."

He laughed. "Okay, I'll do a benefit. For sexually abused children. Now, maybe we can agree on that."

"You were sexually abused?"

"Not really. But it was confusing. I've never understood it. My father is so strange."

"All fathers are strange, seems to me."

"Well, your father never let you crawl into bed with him I'll bet."

"No, that he didn't do. I'd be the last one he'd do that with!"

"See. That's the way most fathers feel. What my father felt I'll never know."

"He took you to bed?"

He nodded and sipped some more wine. I was sure he was going to finish the bottle all by himself. "Well, here's what happened. When he had his heart attack and was made to stay home, in his room, I'd go in there. I was only nine and I knew he didn't like me but he cared about me. He'd had a daughter and a son. Both of us had let him down. How I'd let him down was very complex. Maybe he thought I'd never be able to take over the business, that I wasn't strong enough, I don't know. I knew by then that I wanted to sing. I wanted to be a singer and I knew it drove him nuts. The more nuts it drove him, the more I wanted to be singer. " He laughed. "I remember that at the time we had three records in the top ten at once, he called me and told me I'd done good and I just said, 'I couldn't have done it without you' and I meant it. If he hadn't hated what I was doing I never would have done it.

"But, anyway, I could sense his breathing change as I stepped near him. He brushed his hair back and sat up, as if I was some important company. And he asked me to sit with him on the bed and look out, over the land, his land, the miles and miles that we own there, and he told me not to say anything, just sit there next to him. And I would cut school to be able to do that, go in his room and sit in bed with him, and pretty soon he had his arm around me and then once he said, 'I can't stand what you are, you know that? But I can't do anything for you. I can't do anything for anyone anymore.' And we'd watch the sun setting in the west across the fields like it was a show. And he would hug me, hug me so hard I could hear the thudding of his weak old heart and he would complain about mother and the people who worked for him and everything and say how nobody loved him. All the while, he would run his hands up and down my body. It gave me the creeps.

"And then he asked me why I came every day and I said I hadn't anything better to do. He shook his head in disgust and said that wasn't a nice thing to say but it was nice of me to come just the same."

"And what happened?"

"He got well and was as mean and awful as ever. We never talked about those days and I was never so close to him again."

"Still, it wasn't so bad -"

"What was bad was that I wanted him, you know, in a sexual way, and I know he knew it. That's what disgusted him. He knew my secret. Nobody knew my secret, but he knew. That's why I played football, just to please him."

"You too? I tried it, but I was always too little. I can remember Pa'd yell across the field at me, 'You're standin' up, get low,' or 'Keep your hands in, stupid!' If I knew he was going to be there, I found something else to do. That would even make him madder. Finally I quit altogether. Then he said, 'Just as well, you'd never be anything more 'n a benchwarmer. Just a goddamn benchwarmer.' It was great."

"Mine called me scum. Always called me 'scum of the earth.' Maybe I am. Who knows. I know he thought there was nothing in the world worse than being a sissy."

"Maybe it takes one to know one, ever think of that?"

"Yes, it's crossed my mind. He's probably this mean nasty man 'cause he's never had any and he's always wanted it!" He was laughing, but crying, too. "I overheard him say once that he couldn't believe he'd given birth to a son like that." Now he was crying full out. He came into my arms. "Hey, kid, you fuck me tonight, okay? I gotta feel it, and you holding me while you're doing it. Just hold me all night."

"Okay." I didn't tell him but I wanted to hold him forever.

*

He was late waking up the next day. I had fixed breakfast and was eating it when he stood in the doorway with a huge erection. He didn't say anything, just started stroking it.

"My turn?" I asked, munching my Cheerios.

He just smiled. I put down my spoon and silently moved past him onto the bed. I lay on my stomach and lifted myself up to him.

I had greased myself the night before, before he told me he wanted to get fucked, and I was ready, but still it hurt when he shoved it in. "Please, it hurts," I groaned.

"Let's try it this way," he said, yanking me over on my back.

I grabbed his arm and pulled him down on me, wrapping my legs around his waist. The small head of his cock slid in easily but the width of it stung the more he shoved. He was enjoying it, gasping as he began to move it inside me but I was still in pain. I rolled him over on his back.

And we started again. I guided his cock into me. I could control how deep it went and I got a rhythm going, ramming myself up and down on it, but still it was stinging me. I thought my insides were being torn up. I slowly rose up until the tip of the cock was at the rim of my asshole, then he began moving his hips, driving himself into me. I cried out in pain but he kept on until I felt a gusher of sperm entering me and he was shaking me.

"Oh, god, kid, god, god..." His voice trailed off as he sucked on my nipples, his spit soaking my chest.

My ass burned as his cock slid from the opening with a terrible pop. I could feel my bowels loosening and I tried to stand up. I felt dizzy. He looked at me, at himself and the bed. "Shit," he said. "What did I do?"

"Nothing. It'll be all right."

His cock and the sheet were covered with blood. "No, you won't. You're hurt. I've hurt you. Damn!" He helped me into the bathroom and washed off my skin, then his cock. "I'm sorry, kid."

"Don't worry about it. Just too much too soon, I guess."

"Fuckin' story of my life. I can't get enough and I take too much. Shit!" He slammed the wall on his way out the door.

Now there was no cheering him up. It seemed like the flood of all the memories, all the talking, maybe even his new position of being the fucker, and a ugly, messy fuck besides, had changed him and our relationship. He started drinking early and wouldn't stop. The wine was all gone but he'd brought plenty of his Jack Daniels. The more he drank, the more difficult be became. Finally, I stopped talking. I couldn't watch him just keep on drinking, out of control. I went outside and sat on the little porch. It began to rain, hard. I was miserable. My ass ached. My heart ached. I wanted to leave, but I was stuck there, with him. Finally, I begged him to take me home.

"Yeah," he said, slamming the bottle of bourbon on the table and switching off the television, "let's get the fuck outta here. I can't stand it here. I never could. I don't know why we came."

As he began to stand, I thought he might fall over but he didn't. He pulled himself together and said it: "Dammit, I can't stand being stuck here with a fucking fairy."

I felt like saying, "Dammit, man, I hate being stuck here with a fucking drunk!" But I didn't. I decided it was all my fault. I'd wanted him to be the one to fuck me. I had let him fuck me. He loved it; couldn't get enough. But that was when he was sober. After something to drink, I had turned into something he despised. I had turned into the thing he hated more than anything else: a fairy. He looked at me and saw himself.

Now I hated myself again. I'd been seduced by the dream that I was his lover, a strange kind of surrogate wife, another person that he had shared his most intimate secrets with and he was now regretting it. I had gone beyond what was intended, that I simply serve a purpose, a live-in whore to relieve his tension when he was bored after a long day at the studio. I wanted to go back to the house in the hills, to the way we were before I'd been so stupid. I wanted to go, rush back, back to the time before reality had set in, as it always has a way of doing.

And I didn't realize just how intoxicated Joe was until he started the car and we turned onto the main road. On the way up the mountain, it had been fun, seeing how fast we could take the blind curves. But going down, now, with him stoned, with the roads slick from the rain, I became terrified. If only I'd known how to drive. I had learned how to read, next was driving school. But a lot of good that did now.

I begged him to slow down. There were two hairpin curves in front of us and I looked down the mountain and for a second, through the mist, I thought I saw another car coming up on the wrong side of the road. The speedometer was hitting seventy and the second blind curve approached. Joe twisted the wheel to the right like a crazy man and we spun toward the edge of the gravel but not in time to get out of the way of the car coming up the mountain, a projectile whizzing toward us. Joe hit the accelerator, trying to get away. As the other car slammed into us, we went into a skid and I screamed...

From the LP "I Remember You"/Sung by Joe Skinner/Side 2, Cut 8, (Reprise) "I Remember You:" "...When my life is through / And the angels ask me to recall / That thrill of them all / Then I shall tell them / I remember you."

They put me in a room alone. I could barely lift my arms so I kept the remote control for the TV on the bed next to my hand. I never saw a report on the accident. Benny had arranged everything and Joe was being flown back to Alabama on the company plane for burial. I wouldn't be going. I wasn't invited, of course, but I would have to stay in the hospital for at least a week.

"You're lucky that old car didn't have seat belts," Benny said when he finally came to see me. "You were thrown from the damn car and ended up in some trees. Joe wasn't so lucky. He had massive internal injuries. The steering wheel..." he started sobbing. I felt even sorrier for him than for myself. He loved Joe more than I ever could, I decided, and never got to express it physically.

"Get some rest," he said after he pulled himself together. Patting my leg, he smiled and said, "I'll see you tomorrow."

Rest, shit. At that moment I wanted to die. Seeing Benny crying, remembering the past few months, how wonderful it had been. If I hadn't insisted we go home, none of it would have happened. It was all my fault.

Like when I was ten and my father got drunk and told me it was my fault Mom had died. Tumors on the brain were my fault. I must have caused them, I figured.

And then I begged him to take me camping with him. At first it was great; we took the old canoe and slept in tents. We ate off the land, wild plants and berries, and caught fish and fried them.

One afternoon we stalked through the thick wood, alive to every sound and movement. Suddenly, a rabbit appeared, its summer coat of brown turning white for winter. "Hey, the Easter bunny," I whispered to my father. But my father didn't even smile. He told me we could have it for dinner that night if I could hit it with my .22. I did, catching it just below the eye.

My father applauding, I rushed up to it. It lay impossibly still. The eyes were still open and a trickle of blood came from one eye, like a tear. I'd tracked animals only to watch them, never to kill them. I began to cry. My father called me a "goddamn sissy." I couldn't eat that night. I'd killed the Easter bunny. It was all my fault.

*

"What's this?" I asked Benny a couple of days later as he handed me a legal-looking document with all kinds of copies and a gold pen. He said he was on his way to Alabama for the memorial service and he wanted to take the documents to the Skinners.

"This is an agreement that you'll never speak about this, any of it, ever." He called in a nurse to be a witness.

I signed all the copies without reading them and handed them back to him.

"You didn't read it."

"Doesn't matter anymore, does it?"

He dismissed the nurse and closed the door. "What it says is that you get Joe's condo in Maui," he cleared his throat, "and $50,000 a year for 10 years."

"That's a lot more than I deserve. I never should have let him drive - "

"Stop that shit!" He shoved the papers in his briefcase then looked up at me again. "And now that it doesn't matter you should know the truth."

"Yeah?"

"The reason Joe hated himself so much."

"Oh?"

"That night, the night Paulie died, Joe arranged for the boy and sent him to Paulie with some drugs. Joe wasn't there. He was with Luisa like he said, but he bought the deal and he could never forgive himself."

"I thought so. That's why you were so pissed when I did that arranging for Rodney." And I closed my eyes and began to play all the tapes over again in my mind.

"Yes," he said, starting to leave, but then he came back and stood beside my hospital bed. I opened my eyes and he looked deep into them. "You're lucky to be alive, you know that?"

"Yes."

"And there's no permanent damage. Oh, maybe some scars on your legs, but nothing permanent."

"Yeah, nothin' permanent."

"You'll be just as gorgeous as ever." He smiled. "You know, I'd like to come see you in Maui."

"Sure, Mr. Kaplan. Anything you say." I smiled back. "Anything."

"I'll hold you to that, kid." And he began making his way out of the room.

I nodded and felt like saying, "Hey, you got my signature, Mr. Kaplan. You got my fucking signature," but I didn't. I just thought, Once a whore, always a whore. But then I chuckled to myself thinking, But hey, I'm probably the best damn whore there ever was, and I knew for a little kid like me that had to count for something.

Epilogue

For the first couple of months on Maui, I waited for Benny. But he was always too busy to fly over and I was growing more and more restless.

It was a beautiful place but I was bored out of my mind. I'd sent my father a postcard every day and I was running out of things to say. He probably didn't believe for a second I was writing him anyway so it didn't really matter.

At least I'd learned to drive. I rented a jeep and drove all over, taking the Kahekili Highway faster than anybody else ever had, at least that's what the gasping instructor said. Instead of letting the accident get to me, I'd decided never to ride with anyone else again. I would do all the driving myself.

And then one day, out of the blue, Rodney showed up.

"I need your help," he said, still panting from the walk from the parking lot.

"Oh."

"Benny destroyed all the discs. 'There'll be no book,' he said. That's what the bastard said, 'No book.'"

"That's right, there'll be no book."

"But it was so important to Joe."

"No, not really. He was never going to let you tell the truth, you know that. And without being able to do that, what's the point?"

"But that's the whole idea. Now I want to tell the truth."

"Go ahead. I can't. I've signed a contract."

"I've thought about that. What if I wrote the book about you?"

"Me? What good is that? I'm nobody."

"Ha! You nearly died with him. You're somebody now. That's why Benny's parked you over here so no one can find you."

"Sure," I said.

He had made reservations at the Marriott but I told him he could stay the night, in the guest bedroom, if he bought me dinner. He smiled, "It's a deal."

I helped him carry in his luggage and then I told him he could take me to dinner at the Swan Court in the Hyatt Regency, one of the most expensive places on the Island. We had to dress and I really laughed when he said I looked so "grown up" in my Polo outfit I'd worn in New York.

I'd only been to the Hyatt once, to see the swans in the lagoon. I'd had a drink in the bar and Jim Nabors was there and sent me a second one. Although I wanted to show my appreciation to him for selling Joe the condo, I just nodded my thanks and went home. I wondered if he knew who I was. Maybe he'd seen my picture in *People* when they reported the accident. It was the only picture of me that was published; the photographer, Strange, had sold it to 'em. They cropped it at my navel and called me a "former model," which was a lot better than some of the other things they could have said. And then in the article they said I was Joe's "bodyguard." Obviously, good old Benny took care of it.

...At dinner, with wine in me, I became more agreeable to Rodney's plan, and to Rodney.

"We'd have a business relationship," he said, cutting his blackened mahi mahi.

"That's about all I seem to ever have."

He smiled. "Is that what you were? I never really knew, you know."

"Only for a few months. I didn't work the streets, though. I had an agent and a beeper. You do what you gotta do. But once you do, nobody will let you forget it."

"I understand. But I can forget things easily. I'm a forgiving man."

"I'm glad of that, believe me." He was beaten and robbed. It was all my fault.

He looked away and sipped his wine, not wanting to get his hopes up I suppose. But the more wine I drank, the better he looked. I was horny for some contact with another human. I realized I hadn't had sex with anybody but myself for weeks. Although I'd had plenty of opportunities every time I went down to Makena Beach, I kept thinking about Joe and missing him. And I kept telling myself I was saving it up for Benny, figuring it was part of the deal, but obviously I was wrong; Benny was too busy counting his royalties to worry about a piece of ass.

"I really can't cooperate with you," I told Rodney. "On a book, that is. Not openly, anyway. See, I don't want to fuck up this deal with Benny and the Skinner family."

"I understand. But I don't see any harm in your just reconstructing what was on the discs. I could say I memorized it all."

"I'll see," I said, dropping a couple of hundreds on the tray with the bill.

"But - "

I held up my hand. "This one's on the Skinners."

*

When we returned to the condo, Rodney treated me as if I was a piece of sculpture, wanting nothing more from me than to let him worship me. And I only wanted to be nice to him, to make up for my stupidity. Like I said, I learned a long time ago a lot can depend on a little.

I'd been with so many johns one more or less didn't seem to matter, but when he had removed all my clothes and was kissing me, kissing me everywhere, I gave myself up to the moment and asked what he enjoyed most. When he said he really got off on what he so seldom got, a good fuck, I told him he'd come to the right island.

It had to be in the dark for me to pull it off, but he didn't mind. "I don't think I can take it," he said as I began, carefully, slowly sliding it in.

"Sure you can," I said.

And he did. They always said that and they always took it all, all the way down to my pubes.

He loved it so much, groaning, screaming, heaving himself up to meet every stroke, that I came after about five minutes but kept on, turning him over on his back and jerking him off.

When I returned from the bathroom, he was still lying on the bed in a daze, sliding his fingers through the cum on his hairy belly.

"You are incredible," he sighed. "Did you do that to Joe Skinner?"

"Can't say."

"But you have to. That kind of fuck has to be immortalized, in a book."

I laughed. "Hey, just make it up. Doesn't matter anymore, does it? He's gone and nobody'd believe me anyway. Just make it up."
*

The next day, I took him to Haleakala Crater.

"Ya gotta see it," I said as we bounced along the mountain road in my jeep. "It's one of the biggest in the whole world."

He chuckled, "Yeah, I'm beginning to like 'em big." And he dropped his hand into my crotch and left it there. It felt good; I had missed adoration.

In the late afternoon, we stood at the Leleiwi Overlook, six miles up, and I held his arm. "Isn't this weird?"

And what they call "The Specter" occurred, our shadows showing up on the heavy cloud layer with a rainbow around them.

"Wonderful," he said, slipping his arm around my waist and hugging me to his tall, bulky body. "Simply wonderful."

And in that moment I realized I really liked Rodney. I didn't love him, not like I did Joe. But I liked him. He was so caring, so happy when he was with me. I began to think about the other men, that maybe if I'd given them a chance, some more time, maybe I would have liked them, too.

"I love you," Rodney whispered in my ear.

I chuckled, "You'll get over it."

Rodney stayed three days and when he was leaving he said, "I'll be back."

"I know."

"But I've gotta give it a rest," he groaned, "Shit, I won't be able to sit down for weeks."

"Ha! You'll get used it. My pa always said you can get used to anything."

He stopped, dropped his bag, and took me in his big arms. "I sure could get used to this."

And I closed my eyes and remembered that song, that album, that man. And was glad I'd turned down Rodney's offer. He could say what he wanted about Joe; it didn't matter. That's what they do, Benny said, after a star has died; they are free to make up anything they want.

But I was lucky. I didn't need to make anything up. Shit, I'd been there.

The Lyricists of
Joe Skinner's Songs of Love

"I Remember You:" Copyright and Lyrics by Johnny Mercer

"I Won't Send Roses:" Copyright and lyrics Jerry Herman.

"Easy to Love:" Lyrics by Cole Porter (Copyright by Chappell & Co.)

"Unforgettable:" Lyrics by Irving Gordon (Copyright by Bourne Music)

"I Could Get Used to This:" Lyrics by Ellen Silverstein (Copyright by Wild Pink Music and Never Off Key)

"What a Difference A Day Makes:" Lyrics by Maria Grever (Copyright by E. B. Marks Music/BMI)

"Impossible:" Copyright and lyrics by Steve Allen.

"Fairy Tales:" Lyrics by Anita Baker (Copyright by All Baker's Music)

"More Than You Know:" Lyrics by Anita Baker (Copyright by All Baker's Music)

"A Time for Love:" Lyrics by Paul Francis Webster (Copyright by M. Whitmark & Sons)

"Don't Explain:" Recorded by Robert Palmer, written by Holiday/ Herzog (Copyright by EMI USA)

"Let's Get Lost:" Copyright and lyrics by Jimmy McHugh.

Acknowledgements

I wish to thank Joe Leslie for his invaluable contribution to this book. His story, "Fresh," originally appeared in our anthology "A Natural Beauty" and served as the inspiration for "The Kid."

As the story developed, Joe, being an educator of many years standing, provided the background needed to make William's learning problems accurate and as poignant as they are.

I also gratefully acknowledge the assistance of our longtime editor, "Georgia John," and Art & Mike in bringing this story to life.

Thanks, too, to Brown Bag Co., Hollywood, for supplying the beautiful photography for this book.

- John Patrick

Footnote

"A Study in Sexuality:
The Complexity of What We Are"

THOR PRODUCTIONS

Star of Bisexual Videos Chance Caldwell:
"I like men and women and I wanted to be in the movies.
I'm also horny all the time, so I thought, 'Why not?'"

The story you have just read is a study in the complexity of what we are sexually. William, although he had heterosexual encounters, preferred the company of men. He was not the tormented closet case Joe Skinner was. Indeed, the confused sexual feelings Joe had for Paulie, and the fact that he may have contributed to his partner's death, haunted him for the rest of his life. Eventually, he was able to seek out the company of men, but under his own conditions, his own set of circumstances. And he never uses the term "bisexuality" to describe his behavior. He simply is.

But once Joe had experienced gay sex, he joined the many who fluctuate between the gay and straight communities, in different social contexts or at different points in their lives. Many refuse to believe there is such a thing as bisexuality. Alfred Kinsey, the great sexual researcher, thought forcing a label on anyone was unnatural. In his famous 1948 book, "Sexual Behavior in the Human Male," he wrote, "The world is not to be divided into sheep and goats. Everything is not black and white. It is a fundamental taxonomy that nature rarely deals with discrete categories and tries to force facts into separate pigeonholes. The sooner we learn this concerning sexual behavior, the sooner we can reach a sounder understanding of the realities of sex."

The reality is that like homosexuality, bisexuality has been a part of things since before recorded time. In her new book, "Bi Any Other Name," Lani Kaahumanu says: "Literary and visual references to bisexual desire can be found from the Egyptians on down. Some cultures encouraged or accepted homosexuality as a natural precursor to heterosexual marriage. The Greeks developed a formal system of patriarchy around gay desire and intergenerational love; a married man with a young male lover was not unusual."

Perhaps it has more to do with opportunity than anything else. And perhaps we common folk are just finally catching up to what the rich and famous, including the rock stars in this book, have known all along, that boys will be boys and that can be fun. A recent book about Aristotle Onassis claimed that when he was 73 and married to Jackie O he would have two beautiful Italian boys regularly join him on his yacht and play around. Then, when he was finished with them, he would curtly dismiss them, well paid, we assume, for services rendered.

And then there was Johannes, Prince of Thurn und Taxis, who died in December of 1990. He was descended from Mad King

Ludwig of Bavaria and lived up to his heritage, sometimes playing noblesse oblige, sometimes Caligula. With $2.5 billion in the bank, he could afford to be a madcap consort.

John Richardson, author of the best-selling "A Life of Picasso" and a keen observer of what used to be called the jet set, said of Johannes: "Given his hatred of hypocrisy, Johannes made no bones about liking good-looking boys as much as, if not more than, good-looking girls. In the 1950s, he had a long-standing relationship with a handsome young Chicagoan who was far from poor. ("New money, I fear, " Johannes said. "His family did not get to Chicago until after the fire.") Later, there was a French boy, whose socially ambitious parents were constantly upgrading their fictious title, much to the amusement of Johannes. And then in 1979 he dropped in, as he often did, on a Munich milk bar frequented by swinging adolescents ("Schicki-Micki" kids) whom he would try to impress by driving up in a Winnebago and claiming to be a Panamanian waterskiing champion. Instead of picking up a boy, he ended up with a twenty-year-old girl, a distant cousin, the half-Hungarian Countess Mariae Gloria von Schonburg-Glauchau, who would become more familiarly known as 'Princess TNT.'"

It wasn't long before the aging bachelor realized Gloria would make the perfect consort, providing the solution to a major dynastic problem, the need for an heir. And marriage to Gloria, at that time a dynamic drama student, didn't change his sexual orientation or way of life. Gloria was a free spirit who had no problem adjusting to her husband's proclivities. Each went his or her own way, which didn't prevent them from producing a male heir and two daughters.

Besides what Richardson refers to as "childish perversity," Johannes exhibited a subversiveness and black humor that smacked of Dadaism. Like the Dadaists, he wanted to deride and defy conventional morality and trigger anarchic situations. "He put as much calculation, fantasy, and nerve into his effects as the late Charles Ludlam put into his absurdist farces," Richardson noted. Even after his marriage, Johannes continued to anchor his yacht off the gay beach on the Greek island of Mykonos so as to take his more conventional guests ashore and shock them. "Hairdressers galore," he would promise the ladies. He headed unerringly for the epicenter of the action and immediately set about fomenting a row between two petulant boys. "I saw your friend put sand in your tanning cream," he would tell one. "As for what he did to your towel..." In no time, it was reported, fights would be going on all over the beach.

A first-hand observor of high level hijinks is Liz Taylor. She's been linked, romantically and otherwise, with Rock Hudson, Montgomery Clift and notorious cheapskate billionaire Malcolm Forbes, married with children, who gave his tricks a hundred bucks for their time. When further light was shed on Forbes' bisexuality with the publication of the book "The Man Who Had Everything," Liz said: "It's nobody's business what Malcolm's sexual preferences were. It's nobody's concern. I respected him, which means I respected all of his choices, all the way around."

Speaking of all the way around, one wonders how Malcolm or Ari or Johannes would rank on Kinsey's famous scale, rating human sexuality on a scale of zero to six. Homosexuality never crosses the mind of the zeros (appropriately) while the number sixes pretty much know they are completely gay or lesbian early on. Only five percent of the population, Kinsey theorized, live at those ends of the spectrum. The rest are to be found between two and five. The problem with the scale was that it didn't take into account specific life situations, especially those that changed over a period of time. And, no matter how you look at it, you end up with six different "labels."

In my book about Tim Lowe, "Lowe Down," I quote the handsome, always horny star: "I'd love for everyone to forget all the gay and straight shit. I'm a person. That's the reality of it. I don't have time to worry about all these other things, am I this or am I that. Just let me be who I am." And I was content to do just that, with explosive results.

However, one cannot ignore the tendency to label those things we do not understand. Distributors of videos also like to compartmentalize. They like to section their catalogues so customers will be able to easily choose "young stuff" from "he-man stuff" and so on. "Labels are about confusion," Gino Colbert, frequent performer and sometime director of bisexual videos, says. "They get into a whole negative character. You don't need a film that gets into the filmmaker's personal hang ups."

Thanks to video erotica, we are permitted to live vicariously, to see what being bisexual might mean in the sexual arena.

Although lesbian scenes have long been a staple of straight tapes, because it is said men love to watch women eat each other out, films pairing men with each other, and perhaps a woman along for the ride, only started to become a staple of a video library in the early '80s. Colbert, who brought us the bisexual potboilers "The Bi Spy" and "Gidget Goes Bi," says there is a market for this: "People want to see these tapes." He admits that "biphobia" exists even in the adult film industry, though much of it may be based on homophobia. At one awards ceremony, a presenter introduced the category by saying it was for people who hadn't made up their mind what they wanted. Colbert says that he never gets into orgies. "It's usually private, intimate sex. I think I shoot the most normal erotica in the business. The women usually come out ahead in the plot, which is either detective or love stories."

One of the early successes, "Bi-Coastal," remains one of the better efforts in this category. It employs a time-worn "a star is born" theme well developed by director Lancer Brooks, who once was known as Tom DeSimone and made "The Idol," "Skin Deep," and "Bad, Bad Boys" for gay audiences. "Bi Coastal" boasts tiptop production values and chronicles the heart-wrenching adventure of an attractive little blonde waif who goes to Hollywood to live with her boyfriend and finds he's taken a powder. So, what to do? She meets a powerful agent named Vanessa, beautifully played by Pat Manning, and she becomes a top model. "I don't know how I'll ever thank you," she tells the agent. Vanessa smiles and says, "You'll find a way, darling. You'll find a way." And, of course, she does. Eventually, the heroine finds her long-lost boyfriend and, to her initial dismay and eventual bliss, discovers he's got a BOY friend. They all get cozy and, presumably, live happily ever after.

Another classic of this genre is "The Big Switch," released in 1985 from Catalina and Paul Norman's first venture as a director. The orgy sequence which, natch, climaxes the film is frenzied, with every imaginable sex act occurring at least twice. Lots of juice flows in the finale as Tex Anthony plugs Beverly Glenn while he is getting plugged by Mark Miller for the ultimate in bisexual ecstasy. As critic Robert Leighton observed, "Aside from changing sexual tastes, many of the biggest stars of gay films label themsleves straight or bisexual. That these men are all capable of enjoying sex with either men or women is obvious after viewing this production. It's a must for the hard-core voyeur."

One of our favorites from a strictly gay viewpoint is "The Switch

Is On!" written, directed, produced, and photographed by John Travis. The opus employs the same "a star is born" theme as "Bi Coastal" but, unfortunately, doesn't develop it as well. It starts promisingly: Jeff Stryker, in a performance he has yet to top, pun intended, leaves his mother back on the farm and strikes out for Hollywood. His adventures along the way make for some titillating entertainment. Travis is totally in awe of his star and the camera dotes on Stryker. There's lots of sucking on that huge dick and we even have Jeff dancing around in a big shower at a spa and playing on a jungle gym at the beach. And then, sadly, it all ends. They must have run out of money. Surely Travis could have come up with a cozy little ending to this. Couldn't he have had Stryker meeting a producer of gay films and becoming a star overnight, something borrowed from real life? But we'll settle for this as the definitive bisexual Stryker, far superior to his ego-trip "Every Which Way."

Stryker is among the many porn stars who have been forthcoming about their bisexuality in interviews. Jeff says that his cock has "a mind of its own." And with a cock like that, from which the world's most popular dildo was molded, that's understandable.

The hot blond Leo Ford, the popular star of such classic gaymale porn as "Leo & Lance" and "Style," who recently passed away in a motorcyle accident, revealed in an interview that he first became aware of sex in the second grade. One day, at a picnic, he spied a friend of the family who was two years older and couldn't take his eyes off of him. "He was very beautiful," Leo said. "His body was a picture to look at and I was sitting with my grandmother. I remember whispering to her, 'That boy is so beautiful...look how pretty he is.' And my grandmother said, 'That's okay for you to think like that.' I went home and got turned on in my sleep and that's when I first masturbated. I wasn't able to come but I got a tremendous feeling.

"After that, I got into fights in school just so I could touch other boys. I first heard the word 'homosexual' in the sixth grade. I had a girlfriend who had the biggest tits in school. We would draw a lot of goodlooking guys - and there was a boy in school who was very goodlooking, and we were all skipping school together one day. We were in this attic at his mother's house and I had my first experience with this boy. We had something to smoke and the girls fell asleep so we got together at the far end of the attic. He made the first move. He wrote 'bisexual' on my arm. I didn't know what it meant and he said, 'That means you like guys as well as girls.' Then we played with each other and we sucked each other but we didn't get off.

"When my mother saw what was written on my arm, she asked, 'What's this?' And I said, 'Ben wrote that. I don't know what it means.' She didn't say anything. She didn't know what to say. Anyway, the next day, I was sitting in the living room with my brothers and my mother. I guess they were discussing what to do about me. My brother Tom, who's two years older, said, 'Well, it's his long blond hair. He has to get his hair cut.' And then they had the priest talk to me. Nothing did any good." Leo said that for years he would go "in and out," meeting someone who was "this way or that way," and having sex with them. But it was never in a menage a' trois or orgy situation as you might expect given his profession. Rather it was, in the words of the star, "very one on one."

Perhaps to make the sex more universally appealing, the orgy has become a staple of bisexual videos. My collaborator Tim Lowe has the dubious distinction of appearing in perhaps the sleaziest of the bisexual videos to date, made late in his career, "Angels by Day, Devils Bi-Night." My review of the film, as it appeared in "Lowe Down:"

"Tim keeps disappearing in this Eselle (sic) Ferrand production for Filmco and it's easy to see why. This is arguably the sleaziest video Tim ever made. The ladies (and I use that term loosely) are Bianca, Sharon Kane, Cassi Nova, Kay Sera and Rusty Chaps (no kiddin', those are the stage names). The men include Rod Garreto, Marc Radcliffe, Eric Von Buelow (no kiddin'). The premise: nurses by day run an 'emergency hotline' by night.

"Tim, studily dressed in jeans and a black tank top, and Marc drop by the girls' apartment. 'What perverted things you tellin' the customers now?' Tim asks. '...To add another man to their lovemaking,' one of the sluts replies. 'What's so strange about that?' Marc asks. Tim interjects: 'What Robert (Marc's name in this little play) means is that everyone must fantasize about it every now and then. Doesn't it kinda drive you crazy, make your nipples hard?' 'Are you crazy?' one girl laughs 'Are you kiddin' me? That's my all-time fantasy, watching two guys suck each other's cock!' 'You mean, like this?' Tim asks, zipping down Marc's pants and taking out his limp salami and jamming it in his mouth. But Marc, alas, can't get it up so he goes to Tim's crotch while Tim gives one of the babes a tongue-lashing: 'Your pussy tastes fucking good,' Tim sighs. But soon it's back to Marc's dick while one of the girls goes down on him. But Marc still can't get it hard, so Tim just lays back and enjoys it as Marc and a girl take turns sucking him. Finally, Tim slips on a rubber and fucks one of the girls but before long he's disappeared and Marc is getting finger fucked by the girls. Just as suddenly, Tim comes back (did he have to relieve himself? What's happening here?) and slips it to Marc. Tim cums, then disappears again, leaving hapless Marc to fend for himself.

"The last scene of this tedious video is the obligatory orgy and this one is held at a bar on a slow night, with customers in attendance, billed in the credits as 'The Bad Boys at the Bar, including Bruce Seven as himself.' We find Tim on stage alongside a light-skinned black (Rick Wynn), holding the black's cock while a blonde goes down on it. Then Tim disappears again while the black screws the blonde. Later, Tim comes back to screw her himself. We don't see any more of this because the action shifts to the bar where Marc is nibbling on the balls of studly Jake Larkin who is getting fucked with a string of beads. Mercifully, the whole thing simply ends and as the end title is shown, the camera pulls back to show the director and, at her side, is Tim, arms crossed, chatting with her. Perhaps that's where he was all the time, picking up pointers for a future career behind the cameras? If so, by watching this filming he certainly learned what to avoid."

Some porn stars claim they are manipulated into gay sex. In William Higgins' hugely popular 1985 release, "The Young & The Hung," gorgeous Chris Lance swaps blow-jobs with Brian Estevez (billed as Mike Raymond) through a hole. Later, after bottoming for many stars, Brian would confess: "They told me I wasn't big enough or buff enough to play a top role, so I was labeled a bottom - a small hot guy who gets dick up his ass." Now does that sound like a bisexual to you?

It doesn't to me either, but listen as Brian tells us just what it all means to him: "I jack off, even with men, you know. I can enjoy sex with a man, after doing all the movies and breaking down and breaking the ice and breaking through the sexuality thing...and the fear and everything else. If I chose to do it, I can enjoy it. It's just my genes, inside of me, something inside of me...I prefer women."

But he says he was lucky to have done the movies. "This one producer, I'm not going to say who, always says to me, 'You fucking love it -you love that dick in your ass.' He wants me to say, 'Okay, I love it! I love it!' Look, when I started out there was the pain. I was just doing it without any emotion or feeling, then as time went on, I started to let myself relax and enjoy. I mean, eventually you get honest with yourself. Sure, it does feel good, the prostate is a gland. If you massage it, of course you'll feel good. Anybody's gonna feel good. I don't care if a guy says he's the straightest guy in the world and that it doesn't do anything for him or make him feel good - if you stick a finger up his ass and rub his prostate, and he doesn't say it feels good - what's wrong with this guy? I always hear it in the business, 'Oh, I'm straight.' Then, all the gay men go: 'You're a fucking liar - you're not any straighter than we are.' It's all crazy. I don't know. I guess at this point I have to say I'm bisexual."

As renowned gaymale film critic Dave Kinnick has remarked: "It's always interesting to see someone actually coming out while in the process of making gay pornographic films. I've seen it happen a lot and it's so weird - like stripping gears on a car."

As a longtime fan of video erotica, it has been a personal source of fascination to watch boys work out their sexual confusion while making porn films. Perhaps they use it as an excuse to indulge, conveniently slipping back into a "straight persona" when the task is done.

The popular dancer and porn star Damien ("Buttbusters" and "Read My Lips") commented: "Yeah, I mean once you've done that, what is there? You're out." Being "out," if that is what it is really, is what it's all about, it seems. But even Damien, who fully admits to being gay, not bi, won't get fucked on screen. "I've never bottomed because personally it's something that is really important to me. I know it sounds stupid but in my personal life there have only been three people who have done that to me, the last being my current lover (the former porn star Tony Sinatra, a.k.a. Erickson). I couldn't even tell you what it would take for me to bottom in a movie."

When he had only two movies out, he was amazed at the incredible amount mail he got. "This is the first one I ever got, right after 'Read My Lips' came out. This guy says, 'You're a stud -a near flawless example of gentle/ masculine beauty.' Isn't that fabulous?"

"When I started out," Cameron Kelly, veteran of dozens of

gay porn films said, "when it came to sex, I had no real preferences. I just liked sex in general and I was pretty much willing to do anything for adventure." And Adam Grant, king of the sequels, including "Two Handfuls II," "Head of the Class II," and "Sailor in the Wild II," is another of this new breed of sexual athlete, able to deal with whatever comes up. Says he: "I like women, I like men. I never really put much a label on it. I'm just a very sexual being."

Another "very sexual being" is porn star Chance Caldwell, who toils in Colbert's "Bi Madness" and Catalina's "Sex Bi Lex." A former wrestler and truck driver from Czechoslovakia, Caldwell says: "I always felt this way, since I was 13. I like men and women and I wanted to be in movies. I'm horny all the time, so I thought, 'Why not? It's more variety. It's something different.'"

The fact that Chance grew up on foreign soil provides a clue to his openness.

As Grace Jones commented, "In America, bisexuality is such a big deal. Americans are so wrapped up in what is normal, what is right and pure. The only things that are pure are sex and nature. Nature doesn't argue back, it just is. It survives and evolves and returns."

Speaking of evolving, the scholar Arthur Evans, author of "The God of Ecstasy," describes the Athenian man, raised to be a warrior, the man who is now most likely to be considered homophobic, as one whose values are counter to many deeply rooted human capacities. States the author: "We are not born exclusively masculine or feminine, nor alienated from nature, nor inclined toward perpetual violence to the members of our species. On the contrary, we all have the capacity for a very wide spectrum of human characteristics, as evidenced by the glorious variety in values and behavior found in the world's differing cultures. But when we are raised in a society that deliberately delineates half of the spectrum of human abilities and feelings as taboo, every person born into that society is fated to spend a huge amount of energy denying half of his or her personality."

In America's appallingly sex-negative society, author Kaahumanu summarizes it best: "We must identify the complexity of what we are."

Afterword:
"The Hidden Handicap"

By Joe Leslie

William, the protagonist in this novel, "The Kid," possesses a "hidden handicap," a reading disorder eventually diagnosed as dyslexia.

Experts cannot even agree on a standard definition of this disability. Sylvia Farnham-Diggory, in her book "Structural Approaches to Dyslexia," published by the Harvard Press, states: "Offering a definition of dyslexia amounts to 'waving a red flag in front of a herd of bulls.' Parents and professionals alike. Far from clarifying the situation, the definition (inspires) so much snorting and ground-pawing that the conceptual dust has grown thicker than ever. Definitions are not truth: they merely set up the conditions under which particular actions are to be taken. Some of these actions may be experiments, some of which may produce results that have bearing on truth, but the definitions simply name the game."

Further, as Susan Spaeth Cherry, author of "Dyslexia: The Hidden Handicap," asserts, some learning experts even doubt that dyslexia exists, arguing that "a diagnosis of the disorder lumps together various causes of poor reading. Many schools ignore the specialized needs of dyslexics by dumping them into classrooms for children with multiple handicaps."

A lack of understanding of his abnormality on the part of parents and teachers can have a severe impact on a disabled youngster's self-worth. The ultimate irony of the story of "The Kid" is that while his parents and teachers condemned him, not recognizing his other qualities, such as his physical beauty, honesty, integrity and eventual virility, these attributes would be those that would serve him well during the time we are fortunate enough to meet up with him. And it is those qualities that come to fascinate the character of Joe, who becomes William's white knight, and cause him to fall in love with the youth.

Unfortunately, in the real world, for most dyslexics there is no millionaire rock star to lend a helping hand, no white knight, no fairy tale ending. Rather, because of tight budgets, lack of properly trained diagnosticians, and contemptuous administrators and instructors, the dyslexic generally doesn't get the help he needs. And worried and over-protective parents seem to be more at fault than anyone.

Cherry says, "Parents frequently find the dyslexic's conduct baffling, embarrassing and exasperating. Some blame themselves for their youngster's problem; others feel victimized by them."

Cheery quotes Joan Sharpe of Chicago, a mother of two dyslexics: "Having a dyslexic child is very threatening to parents' egos. There were years I felt like a failure."

This feeling of failure manifests itself in a variety of ways, most often overtly, sometimes non-verbally, but almost always in an accusatory way. Many times, those parents who do seek solutions do so to assuage their own anger and frustration rather than to aid the child, who remains a victim until some outside force intercedes to provide aid and comfort.

After reading "The Kid," one of STARbooks' long-time editors recalled: "I had a boyfriend once who, ironically, was named Billy, and he suffered the same problem as the boy in this book. I remember he would hand me a record label and ask, 'What does this say?' just because he didn't want to make the effort to read it. In the story, when William is left alone at the star's hilltop mansion, he is eager to find out about this mystery person and consequently makes an effort to read the CD covers. Later, when he is handed the tabloid, he freezes when confronted with masses of oppressive gray type. He could have made an effort to read it but it would have taken considerable time and effort, and surely Joe would have caught on. What William didn't realize is that Joe's sister had suffered the same problem and been helped by therapy."

Indeed, as we see in "The Kid," a loved one's understanding, coupled with the correct therapy, can not only help a youngster deal with the problem but also have a dramatic impact on his self-esteem. As Sharpe says, "Therapy makes all the difference in the world. It doesn't make the problem go away but it helps the child deal with the problem better."

For further information on specific language disability, you are invited to write: Ms. Rosemary Bowler, Orton Dyslexia Society, 724 York Road, Baltimore MD 21204, or call (301) 296-0232.

"The Book of the Year"*
is now even bigger, even better!

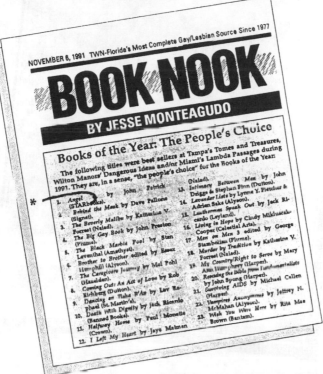

NOVEMBER 6, 1991 TWN-Florida's Most Complete Gay/Lesbian Source Since 1977

BOOK NOOK
BY JESSE MONTEAGUDO

Books of the Year: The People's Choice

The following titles were best sellers at Tampa's Tomes and Treasures, Wilton Manors' Dangerous Ideas and/or Miami's Lambda Passages during 1991. They are, in a sense, "the people's choice" for the Books of the Year:

1. *Angel* by John Patrick (STARbooks).
2. *Behind the Mask* by Dave Pallone (Signet).
3. *The Beverly Malibu* by Katherine V. Forrest (Naiad).
4. *The Big Gay Book* by John Preston (Plume).
5. *The Black Marble Pool* by Stan Leventhal (Amethyst).
6. *Brother to Brother* edited by Essex Hemphill (Alyson).
7. *The Caregivers Journey* by Mel Pohl (Hazelden).
8. *Coming Out: An Act of Love* by Rob Eichberg (Dutton).
9. *Dancing on Tisha B'Av* by Lev Raphael (St. Martin's).
10. *Death With Dignity* by Jack Ricardo (Banned Books).
11. *Halfway Home* by Paul Monette (Crown).
12. *I Left My Heart* by Jaye Maiman

13. *Intimacy Between Men* by John Driggs & Stephan Finn (Dutton).
14. *Lavender Lists* by Lynne Y. Fletcher & Adrien Saks (Alyson).
15. *Leathermen Speak Out* by Jack Ricardo (Leyland).
16. *Living in Hope* by Cindy Mikluscak-Cooper (Celestial Arts).
17. *Men on Men 3* edited by George Stambolian (Plume).
18. *Murder by Tradition* by Katherine V. Forrest (Naiad).
19. *My Country/Right to Serve* by Mary Ann Humphrey (Harper).
20. *Reading the Bible from Fundamentalists* by John Syong (Harper).
21. *Surviving AIDS* by Michael Callen (Harper).
22. *Vampires Anonymous* by Jeffrey N. McMahan (Alyson).
23. *Wish You Were Here* by Rita Mae Brown (Bantam).

The New International Edition
with even more great reading is here...

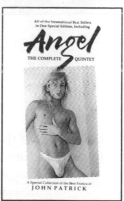

All of the International Best Sellers in One Special Edition, Including

Angel
THE COMPLETE QUINTET

A Special Collection of the Best Erotica of
JOHN PATRICK

141

When having it all is not enough...

No one can say "no" to Angel...

A Special Collection of the Best Erotica of
JOHN PATRICK
Including:

The Romans á Clef
Angel: The Complete Quintet
The Bigger They Are
The Younger They Are
The Harder They Are
Stacy's Story
Stacy's Return

Billy & David: A Deadly Minuet

The Erotic Fables
The Boy in the Park
The Biting Tongue
The Masterpiece

The Star Essays
Excerpts from the Best-Selling Series from
STARbooks, Including:
Christopher Atkins: Chickenhawk's Delight
Vince Cobretti: A Charmed Life
Tim Lowe: Lowe Down
Tom Steele: Hard As Steele
Joey Stefano: Sex Maniac

**International
Edition Includes
Material Never Before
Published**

About the Author

John Patrick is a prolific, prize-winning author of fiction and non-fiction. One of his short stories, "The Well," was honored by PEN American Center as one of the best of 1987, and became the basis for the book "The Bigger They Are," now part of his "Angel: The Complete Quintet," which has become an international best-seller. The author's other acclaimed romans a' clef, "Billy & David: A Deadly Minuet," "Strip: He Danced Alone," and "The Kid," as well as his unique series of erotic books about gay icons, including "The Best of the Superstars," "A Charmed Life: Vince Cobretti," "Lowe Down: Tim Lowe," and "Legends: The World's Sexiest Men," as well as his new non-fiction novel, "What Went Wrong? When Boys Are Bad & Sex Goes Wrong," continue to gain him new fans every day.

A member of the American Booksellers Association, American Civil Liberties Union and the American Booksellers Foundation for Free Expression, the author is the divorced father of two children and now resides on an island in Florida.